50 African Stew Recipes for Home

By: Kelly Johnson

Table of Contents

- West African Peanut Stew
- Jollof Rice with Chicken
- Moroccan Lamb Tagine
- Nigerian Egusi Soup
- South African Bobotie
- Ghanaian Groundnut Soup
- Ethiopian Doro Wat (Spicy Chicken Stew)
- Cape Malay Lamb Curry
- Tanzanian Fish Stew
- Kenyan Sukuma Wiki
- Algerian Chorba
- Senegalese Thieboudienne (Fish and Rice)
- Tunisian Chickpea Stew
- Malawian Nsima with Beef Stew
- Cameroonian Ndolé (Bitterleaf Stew)
- Libyan Shorba (Lamb and Vegetable Stew)
- Zimbabwean Peanut Butter Stew
- Ivorian Kedjenou (Chicken Stew)
- Eritrean Zigni (Spicy Beef Stew)
- Sierra Leonean Cassava Leaf Stew
- Moroccan Harira (Tomato and Lentil Soup)
- Somali Suqaar (Beef Stew)
- Namibian Oxtail Stew
- Rwandan Chicken and Plantain Stew
- Egyptian Molokhia Stew
- Sudanese Bamia (Okra Stew)
- Beninese Gbegiri (Bean Soup)
- Cape Verdean Catchupa (Corn Stew)
- Gabonese Poulet Nyembwe (Chicken in Palm Nut Sauce)
- Burkina Faso's Riz Gras (Rice with Meat and Vegetables)
- Central African Republic's Kanda (Peanut Butter and Spinach Stew)
- Equatorial Guinean Chicken Muamba (Chicken and Palm Butter Stew)
- Guinea-Bissau's Canja de Galinha (Chicken and Rice Soup)
- Lesotho's Moroho (Spinach and Potato Stew)
- Madagascar's Romazava (Meat and Leafy Greens Stew)
- Mauritius' Daube (Beef Stew)

- Mozambique's Matapa (Cassava Leaves and Peanut Stew)
- Niger's Djerma Stew (Beef and Peanut Butter)
- Sao Tome and Principe's Calulu de Peixe (Fish Stew)
- Seychelles' Kat-kat Banane (Plantain Stew)
- South Sudan's Kisra (Sorghum Flatbread) with Stew
- Swaziland's Siswati Stew (Meat and Vegetables)
- Togo's Fufu and Sauce Claire (Peanut Sauce)
- Zambia's Chikanda (Wild Orchid Tubers Stew)
- Botswana's Seswaa (Shredded Beef Stew)
- Comoros' Langouste a la Vanille (Lobster in Vanilla Sauce)
- Djibouti's Fah-fah (Lamb and Yogurt Stew)
- Guinea's Mafé (Peanut Sauce with Meat)
- Kenya's Githeri (Maize and Beans Stew)
- Liberia's Palava Sauce

West African Peanut Stew

Ingredients:

- 2 tablespoons vegetable oil
- 1 large onion, finely chopped
- 3 cloves garlic, minced
- 1 tablespoon grated fresh ginger
- 1 teaspoon ground coriander
- 1 teaspoon ground cumin
- 1/2 teaspoon cayenne pepper (adjust to taste)
- 1 sweet potato, peeled and diced into cubes
- 1 red bell pepper, diced
- 1 can (14 oz) diced tomatoes
- 1 cup vegetable broth or water
- 1 cup smooth peanut butter
- Salt and pepper to taste
- 1 cup chopped spinach or kale (optional)
- Cooked rice, for serving

Instructions:

1. **Sauté Aromatics**: Heat the vegetable oil in a large pot over medium heat. Add the chopped onion and cook until softened, about 5 minutes. Add the minced garlic, grated ginger, ground coriander, cumin, and cayenne pepper. Cook for another 2 minutes until fragrant.
2. **Add Vegetables**: Add the diced sweet potato and red bell pepper to the pot. Stir well to combine with the aromatics.
3. **Simmer**: Pour in the diced tomatoes and vegetable broth (or water). Bring the mixture to a boil, then reduce heat and let it simmer until the sweet potatoes are tender, about 15-20 minutes.
4. **Incorporate Peanut Butter**: Stir in the smooth peanut butter until well combined and the stew is creamy. Adjust the consistency with more broth or water if needed.
5. **Season and Add Greens**: Season with salt and pepper to taste. If using, add chopped spinach or kale and cook for an additional 5 minutes until wilted.
6. **Serve**: Serve the West African Peanut Stew hot over cooked rice. Optionally, garnish with chopped peanuts or fresh cilantro.

This stew is rich, nutty, and spicy, with a perfect balance of flavors from the peanut butter and spices. It's a hearty dish that's often enjoyed with a side of rice or crusty bread.

Jollof Rice with Chicken

Ingredients:

- 2 cups long-grain parboiled rice
- 4 chicken thighs or drumsticks, skin-on
- 1 large onion, finely chopped
- 3 cloves garlic, minced
- 1 red bell pepper, finely chopped
- 1 green bell pepper, finely chopped
- 1 can (14 oz) diced tomatoes
- 2 tablespoons tomato paste
- 1 teaspoon dried thyme
- 1 teaspoon paprika
- 1 teaspoon curry powder
- 1 teaspoon ground cayenne pepper (adjust to taste)
- 2 cups chicken broth or water
- Salt and pepper to taste
- Vegetable oil

Instructions:

1. **Prepare the Chicken**: Season the chicken thighs or drumsticks with salt and pepper. In a large pot or Dutch oven, heat 2 tablespoons of vegetable oil over medium-high heat. Brown the chicken pieces on both sides until golden brown. Remove and set aside.
2. **Sauté Aromatics**: In the same pot, add the chopped onion, garlic, red bell pepper, and green bell pepper. Sauté for about 5 minutes until the vegetables are softened.
3. **Add Tomatoes and Spices**: Stir in the diced tomatoes, tomato paste, dried thyme, paprika, curry powder, and ground cayenne pepper. Cook for another 5 minutes, stirring occasionally, until the mixture is fragrant and slightly reduced.
4. **Simmer with Rice**: Add the parboiled rice to the pot and stir well to coat it with the tomato and vegetable mixture. Pour in the chicken broth or water, and season with salt and pepper to taste. Nestle the browned chicken pieces into the rice.
5. **Cook the Jollof Rice**: Bring the mixture to a boil, then reduce the heat to low. Cover the pot with a lid and let it simmer gently for about 20-25 minutes, or until the rice is cooked through and has absorbed the liquid. Stir occasionally to prevent sticking, and add more broth or water if needed.
6. **Serve**: Once the rice is cooked and fluffy, remove from heat. Fluff the rice with a fork and arrange the chicken pieces on top. Garnish with chopped fresh parsley or cilantro if desired.

Jollof Rice with Chicken is often served hot as a main dish, accompanied by fried plantains, steamed vegetables, or a side salad. It's a comforting and satisfying meal that's enjoyed across many West African countries with variations in ingredients and spices.

Moroccan Lamb Tagine

Ingredients:

- 1.5 lbs (about 700g) lamb shoulder or leg, cut into cubes
- 2 tablespoons olive oil
- 1 large onion, finely chopped
- 3 cloves garlic, minced
- 1 teaspoon ground ginger
- 1 teaspoon ground cumin
- 1 teaspoon ground coriander
- 1 teaspoon ground cinnamon
- 1/2 teaspoon ground turmeric
- 1/2 teaspoon ground paprika
- Pinch of saffron threads (optional)
- Salt and pepper to taste
- 1 tablespoon honey or sugar (optional, for sweetness)
- 1 cup dried apricots, halved
- 1 cup prunes, pitted
- 1/2 cup almonds or other nuts (optional)
- 2 cups chicken or lamb broth
- Fresh cilantro or parsley, chopped (for garnish)
- Cooked couscous or rice (for serving)

Instructions:

1. **Brown the Lamb:**
    - Heat olive oil in a large, heavy-bottomed pot or tagine dish over medium-high heat.
    - Add the lamb cubes in batches and brown them on all sides. Remove and set aside.
2. **Sauté Aromatics:**
    - In the same pot, add chopped onion and garlic. Sauté until softened and lightly golden.
3. **Add Spices:**
    - Add ground ginger, cumin, coriander, cinnamon, turmeric, paprika, saffron (if using), salt, and pepper. Stir well to coat the onions and garlic with the spices.
4. **Simmer the Tagine:**
    - Return the browned lamb to the pot.
    - Add dried apricots, prunes, and nuts (if using).
    - Pour in chicken or lamb broth. Stir to combine.
    - Bring to a boil, then reduce the heat to low. Cover the pot and let it simmer gently for 1.5 to 2 hours, or until the lamb is tender and the flavors have melded

together. Stir occasionally and add more broth or water if necessary to keep it from drying out.
5. **Finish and Serve:**
    - If using honey or sugar for sweetness, stir it in towards the end of cooking.
    - Taste and adjust seasoning if needed.
    - Serve the tagine hot, garnished with chopped fresh cilantro or parsley.
    - Accompany with couscous or rice to soak up the delicious sauce.

Enjoy your Moroccan Lamb Tagine with its rich blend of spices and sweet dried fruits—a perfect dish for special occasions or a comforting meal anytime!

Nigerian Egusi Soup

Ingredients:

- 1 cup egusi (ground melon seeds)
- 1/2 cup palm oil
- 1 medium onion, finely chopped
- 2-3 cups meat or fish (such as beef, goat meat, chicken, or fish), cooked and cut into bite-sized pieces
- 2-3 cups assorted vegetables (e.g., spinach, bitter leaf, pumpkin leaves), chopped
- 2-3 cups broth or water
- 2-3 tablespoons ground crayfish (dried shrimp)
- 2-3 tablespoons ground dried pepper (or to taste)
- Salt to taste
- Seasoning cubes or powder (optional, to taste)
- 1 teaspoon ground uziza seeds (optional, for extra flavor)
- 1/2 cup chopped okra (optional, for added texture)

Instructions:

1. **Prepare the Egusi Paste:**
   - Place the ground egusi seeds in a bowl and gradually add water to make a paste. Stir until smooth and set aside.
2. **Cooking the Soup:**
   - Heat the palm oil in a large pot over medium heat.
   - Add the chopped onions and sauté until translucent.
3. **Add the Egusi Paste:**
   - Reduce the heat to low and carefully add the egusi paste to the pot. Stir continuously to prevent clumping and to evenly distribute the paste with the oil. Cook for about 10-15 minutes, stirring occasionally, until the egusi is slightly fried and the raw taste is gone.
4. **Add Broth and Meat/Fish:**
   - Gradually add the broth or water to the egusi paste, stirring constantly to incorporate and create a smooth consistency.
   - Add the cooked meat or fish pieces to the pot. Allow it to simmer for about 10 minutes to absorb the flavors.
5. **Add Vegetables and Seasonings:**
   - Stir in the chopped vegetables (spinach, bitter leaf, pumpkin leaves) and okra (if using). Cook for another 5-7 minutes until the vegetables are tender but still vibrant.
   - Add ground crayfish, ground dried pepper, salt, and seasoning cubes or powder (if using). Adjust seasoning to taste.
6. **Simmer and Serve:**

- Let the soup simmer gently for another 5-10 minutes to allow all the flavors to meld together.
- If using uziza seeds, sprinkle them over the soup and stir gently.
- Serve hot with a side of pounded yam, fufu, or rice.

Nigerian Egusi Soup is known for its rich, nutty flavor from the egusi seeds, combined with the savory taste of the meat or fish and the vegetables. It's a hearty and satisfying dish enjoyed across Nigeria and beyond.

South African Bobotie

Ingredients:

For the Bobotie:

- 1 kg (2.2 lbs) minced meat (traditionally beef or lamb, or a mixture)
- 2 slices of white bread, soaked in milk
- 2 onions, finely chopped
- 2 cloves garlic, minced
- 2 tablespoons vegetable oil
- 2 tablespoons curry powder
- 1 tablespoon ground turmeric
- 1 tablespoon ground coriander
- 1 tablespoon ground cumin
- 1 tablespoon ground cinnamon
- 2 tablespoons apricot jam (or chutney)
- 1 tablespoon Worcestershire sauce
- 1 tablespoon vinegar (white or apple cider)
- Salt and pepper to taste
- 1/2 cup raisins or sultanas
- 1/4 cup almonds, slivered or chopped (optional)
- 2 tablespoons fresh lemon juice
- 2 bay leaves

For the Egg Custard Topping:

- 3 large eggs
- 1 cup milk
- Pinch of salt

For Serving:

- Cooked rice
- Chutney or salsa

Instructions:

1. **Prepare the Meat Mixture:**
    - Preheat your oven to 180°C (350°F).
    - Heat oil in a large pan over medium heat. Add onions and garlic, sauté until softened.
2. **Add Spices and Meat:**
    - Add curry powder, turmeric, coriander, cumin, and cinnamon to the onions and garlic. Stir for about a minute until fragrant.

- Add minced meat to the pan and cook until browned, breaking up any clumps with a spoon.
3. **Combine Ingredients:**
    - Squeeze excess milk from the soaked bread and add the bread to the meat mixture, stirring to combine.
    - Add apricot jam (or chutney), Worcestershire sauce, vinegar, salt, pepper, raisins or sultanas, and almonds (if using). Mix well.
4. **Simmer and Flavor:**
    - Allow the mixture to simmer gently for about 10 minutes to allow the flavors to meld together.
    - Stir in fresh lemon juice and adjust seasoning if necessary.
    - Remove from heat and transfer the mixture to a greased oven-proof dish. Press bay leaves into the top of the meat mixture.
5. **Prepare the Egg Custard:**
    - In a bowl, beat eggs, milk, and a pinch of salt until well combined.
    - Pour the egg custard mixture evenly over the meat mixture in the dish.
6. **Bake the Bobotie:**
    - Place the dish in the preheated oven and bake for about 30-40 minutes, or until the egg custard is set and golden brown on top.
7. **Serve:**
    - Serve Bobotie hot, accompanied by rice and a side of chutney or salsa.

Bobotie is a wonderfully aromatic dish with a balance of savory, sweet, and spice. It's a true reflection of South African cuisine and is sure to delight your taste buds!

Ghanaian Groundnut Soup

Ingredients:

- 1 cup roasted peanuts, unsalted
- 2 tablespoons peanut oil or vegetable oil
- 1 large onion, finely chopped
- 3 cloves garlic, minced
- 1 inch piece of ginger, grated or minced
- 2 tomatoes, chopped
- 1 teaspoon ground coriander
- 1 teaspoon ground cumin
- 1/2 teaspoon cayenne pepper (adjust to taste)
- 1/2 teaspoon paprika
- 1 teaspoon dried thyme (or use fresh thyme)
- 1 teaspoon ground nutmeg
- 1-2 cups cooked meat or fish (chicken, beef, goat meat, tilapia, or other firm fish), diced or shredded
- 4 cups vegetable or chicken broth
- 1 cup water
- Salt and pepper to taste
- 1/2 cup chopped spinach or kale (optional)
- Cooked rice or fufu, for serving

Instructions:

1. **Prepare the Peanuts:**
    - Grind the roasted peanuts in a food processor or blender until finely ground. Add a little water if needed to help blend into a smooth paste. Set aside.
2. **Sauté Aromatics:**
    - Heat peanut oil in a large pot over medium heat. Add chopped onions and sauté until softened and translucent, about 5 minutes.
    - Add minced garlic and grated ginger. Sauté for another 1-2 minutes until fragrant.
3. **Add Tomatoes and Spices:**
    - Stir in chopped tomatoes and cook until they begin to soften, about 5 minutes.
    - Add ground coriander, cumin, cayenne pepper, paprika, dried thyme, and ground nutmeg. Mix well to combine with the onion and tomato mixture.
4. **Cook the Soup:**
    - Add the ground peanuts (peanut paste) to the pot, stirring continuously to combine with the spices and vegetables.
    - Pour in vegetable or chicken broth and water. Bring the mixture to a boil, then reduce the heat to low.
5. **Simmer and Add Meat/Fish:**

- Add the cooked meat or fish to the pot. Stir well and let the soup simmer gently for about 20-30 minutes, stirring occasionally. This allows the flavors to meld together and the soup to thicken.
    - Season with salt and pepper to taste.
6. **Add Greens (optional) and Serve:**
    - If using chopped spinach or kale, add it to the pot during the last 5 minutes of cooking. Stir until wilted.
7. **Serve:**
    - Serve Ghanaian Groundnut Soup hot, accompanied by cooked rice or fufu.

Enjoy this creamy and flavorful soup that combines the nutty richness of peanuts with a blend of spices and hearty meat or fish. It's a comforting and satisfying dish that reflects the vibrant flavors of Ghanaian cuisine.

Ethiopian Doro Wat (Spicy Chicken Stew)

Ingredients:

For the Spice Paste (Berbere):

- 1/4 cup dried red chili peppers (like New Mexico or Guajillo), seeds removed
- 1/4 cup paprika
- 1 tablespoon ground coriander
- 1 tablespoon ground cumin
- 1 tablespoon ground fenugreek
- 1 tablespoon ground cardamom
- 1 teaspoon ground cloves
- 1 teaspoon ground allspice
- 1 teaspoon ground black pepper
- 1/2 teaspoon ground cinnamon
- 1/2 teaspoon ground nutmeg
- 1/2 teaspoon ground turmeric
- 1/2 teaspoon ground ginger
- 1/4 teaspoon ground ajwain seeds (optional)
- 1/4 teaspoon ground nigella seeds (optional)
- 1/4 teaspoon ground long pepper (optional)
- 1/4 teaspoon ground dried rosemary (optional)
- 1/4 teaspoon ground dried basil (optional)
- 1/4 teaspoon ground dried oregano (optional)

For the Doro Wat:

- 2-3 tablespoons clarified butter (Niter Kibbeh) or regular butter
- 2 large onions, finely chopped
- 4 cloves garlic, minced
- 1 tablespoon fresh ginger, minced
- 2 tablespoons spice paste (Berbere), or to taste (adjust for desired spiciness)
- 2 tablespoons tomato paste
- 2 cups chicken broth or water
- 8-10 chicken drumsticks or thighs, skin-on
- Salt to taste
- 4-6 hard-boiled eggs, peeled
- Fresh cilantro or parsley, chopped (for garnish)
- Injera (Ethiopian flatbread) or rice, for serving

Instructions:

1. **Make the Spice Paste (Berbere):**

- In a dry skillet over medium heat, toast the dried chili peppers for a few minutes until fragrant. Remove from heat and allow to cool.
- Grind the toasted peppers into a fine powder using a spice grinder or mortar and pestle.
- In a bowl, combine the ground chili peppers with all the other spices listed for the Berbere spice mix. Mix well and set aside.

2. **Prepare the Chicken:**
    - Heat the clarified butter (Niter Kibbeh) or regular butter in a large, heavy-bottomed pot over medium heat.
    - Add the chopped onions and sauté until softened and golden, about 8-10 minutes.
    - Stir in the minced garlic and ginger, and sauté for another 2 minutes until fragrant.

3. **Cook the Doro Wat:**
    - Add 2 tablespoons of the Berbere spice paste (adjust to taste) and the tomato paste to the pot. Cook, stirring constantly, for 3-4 minutes to toast the spices and develop flavor.
    - Pour in the chicken broth or water, stirring to combine. Bring the mixture to a simmer.

4. **Add the Chicken:**
    - Season the chicken pieces with salt to taste.
    - Carefully place the chicken pieces into the simmering sauce, ensuring they are submerged.
    - Cover the pot with a lid and let the chicken simmer gently over low heat for about 45 minutes to 1 hour, or until the chicken is tender and cooked through. Stir occasionally.

5. **Finish the Dish:**
    - About 15 minutes before serving, gently add the hard-boiled eggs into the stew, submerging them partially.
    - Taste and adjust seasoning if needed, adding more Berbere paste or salt as desired.

6. **Serve:**
    - Serve Ethiopian Doro Wat hot, garnished with chopped fresh cilantro or parsley.
    - Traditionally, Doro Wat is served with injera (Ethiopian flatbread) to scoop up the stew. Alternatively, you can serve it with rice.

Enjoy the rich, spicy flavors of Ethiopian Doro Wat, a dish that's sure to impress with its complexity and depth of taste!

Cape Malay Lamb Curry

Ingredients:

- 1 kg (about 2.2 lbs) lamb shoulder or leg, cut into cubes
- 2 tablespoons vegetable oil
- 2 onions, finely chopped
- 3 cloves garlic, minced
- 1 tablespoon fresh ginger, grated
- 2 tablespoons Cape Malay curry powder (or regular curry powder if unavailable)
- 1 teaspoon ground turmeric
- 1 teaspoon ground cumin
- 1 teaspoon ground coriander
- 1 cinnamon stick
- 2-3 cardamom pods, lightly crushed
- 2 bay leaves
- 2 tablespoons tomato paste
- 2 cups beef or lamb broth
- 1 cup coconut milk
- 1 tablespoon brown sugar or palm sugar
- Salt and pepper to taste
- 1 cup dried apricots, halved
- Chopped fresh cilantro or parsley, for garnish
- Cooked rice or naan bread, for serving

Instructions:

1. **Brown the Lamb:**
   - Heat the vegetable oil in a large, heavy-bottomed pot over medium-high heat.
   - Add the lamb cubes in batches and brown them on all sides. Remove and set aside.
2. **Sauté Aromatics:**
   - In the same pot, add the chopped onions and cook until softened and translucent, about 5 minutes.
   - Add the minced garlic and grated ginger, and cook for another 1-2 minutes until fragrant.
3. **Add Spices:**
   - Stir in the Cape Malay curry powder, ground turmeric, ground cumin, and ground coriander. Add the cinnamon stick, crushed cardamom pods, and bay leaves. Cook for 1-2 minutes until the spices are fragrant.
4. **Create the Sauce:**
   - Add the tomato paste to the pot and cook, stirring constantly, for 1-2 minutes.
   - Pour in the beef or lamb broth and coconut milk, stirring to combine.
   - Return the browned lamb to the pot. Stir well to coat the meat with the sauce.

5. **Simmer the Curry:**
    - Bring the mixture to a boil, then reduce the heat to low. Cover the pot and let it simmer gently for 1.5 to 2 hours, or until the lamb is tender and the sauce has thickened. Stir occasionally.
    - Taste and adjust seasoning with salt, pepper, and sugar as needed.
6. **Add Dried Apricots:**
    - About 30 minutes before the curry is done, add the halved dried apricots to the pot. Let them simmer in the sauce until plump and softened.
7. **Serve:**
    - Remove the cinnamon stick, bay leaves, and cardamom pods (if you can find them).
    - Serve Cape Malay Lamb Curry hot, garnished with chopped fresh cilantro or parsley.
    - Accompany with cooked rice or naan bread to soak up the delicious sauce.

Enjoy the rich and fragrant flavors of Cape Malay Lamb Curry, a dish that perfectly blends savory spices with the subtle sweetness of dried apricots!

Tanzanian Fish Stew

Ingredients:

- 1 kg (about 2.2 lbs) firm white fish fillets (such as tilapia, snapper, or cod), cut into chunks
- 2 tablespoons vegetable oil
- 1 onion, finely chopped
- 3 cloves garlic, minced
- 1 tablespoon fresh ginger, grated
- 1-2 hot chili peppers (like Scotch bonnet or bird's eye chili), finely chopped (adjust to taste)
- 1 teaspoon ground coriander
- 1 teaspoon ground cumin
- 1 teaspoon ground turmeric
- 1/2 teaspoon ground cinnamon
- 1/2 teaspoon ground cloves
- 1/2 teaspoon ground cardamom
- 1/2 teaspoon ground black pepper
- 1/2 teaspoon paprika
- 1/2 teaspoon ground nutmeg
- 1 bay leaf
- 2 large tomatoes, chopped
- 1 tablespoon tomato paste
- 1 cup coconut milk
- 2 cups fish or vegetable broth
- Juice of 1 lime or lemon
- Salt to taste
- Fresh cilantro, chopped, for garnish
- Cooked rice or chapati, for serving

Instructions:

1. **Sauté Aromatics:**
   - Heat vegetable oil in a large, heavy-bottomed pot over medium heat.
   - Add the chopped onion and sauté until softened and translucent, about 5 minutes.
   - Add minced garlic, grated ginger, and chopped chili peppers. Sauté for another 2 minutes until fragrant.
2. **Add Spices:**
   - Stir in ground coriander, cumin, turmeric, cinnamon, cloves, cardamom, black pepper, paprika, nutmeg, and bay leaf. Cook for 1-2 minutes until spices are fragrant.
3. **Create the Base:**

- Add chopped tomatoes and tomato paste to the pot. Cook, stirring occasionally, until tomatoes start to break down and release their juices, about 5-7 minutes.
4. **Simmer the Stew:**
    - Pour in coconut milk and fish or vegetable broth. Stir well to combine.
    - Bring the mixture to a boil, then reduce the heat to low. Cover the pot and let it simmer gently for about 15-20 minutes to allow flavors to meld together.
5. **Add Fish and Finish:**
    - Carefully add the fish chunks to the stew. Simmer gently for another 10-15 minutes, or until the fish is cooked through and flakes easily with a fork.
    - Stir in lime or lemon juice and season with salt to taste.
6. **Serve:**
    - Remove the bay leaf from the stew.
    - Serve Tanzanian Fish Stew hot, garnished with chopped fresh cilantro.
    - Serve with cooked rice or chapati on the side.

Enjoy the aromatic and flavorful Tanzanian Fish Stew, perfect for a comforting and satisfying meal that highlights the vibrant spices and coconut milk typical of East African cuisine!

Kenyan Sukuma Wiki

Ingredients:

- 1 bunch sukuma wiki (collard greens), washed and chopped
- 2 tablespoons vegetable oil
- 1 onion, finely chopped
- 2 tomatoes, chopped
- 2 cloves garlic, minced
- 1 teaspoon grated ginger
- 1-2 chili peppers, chopped (optional, for heat)
- Salt and pepper to taste
- 1/2 teaspoon ground cumin (optional)
- 1/2 teaspoon ground coriander (optional)
- Juice of 1/2 lemon or lime (optional, for tanginess)
- Cooked meat (like beef or chicken), diced (optional, for added protein)

Instructions:

1. **Prepare the Sukuma Wiki:**
   - Wash the sukuma wiki thoroughly and chop into small pieces, discarding any tough stems.
2. **Sauté Aromatics:**
   - Heat vegetable oil in a large pan over medium heat. Add chopped onion and sauté until softened and translucent, about 5 minutes.
   - Add minced garlic, grated ginger, and chopped chili peppers (if using). Sauté for another 1-2 minutes until fragrant.
3. **Cook Tomatoes and Spices:**
   - Add chopped tomatoes to the pan. Cook, stirring occasionally, until tomatoes are softened and start to break down, about 5-7 minutes.
   - If using, add ground cumin and ground coriander. Stir to combine with the tomatoes and aromatics.
4. **Add Sukuma Wiki:**
   - Add the chopped sukuma wiki to the pan. Stir well to combine with the tomato mixture and coat the greens with the flavors.
   - If using cooked meat, add it to the pan at this point.
5. **Simmer:**
   - Reduce the heat to low, cover the pan, and let the sukuma wiki simmer for about 15-20 minutes, or until the greens are tender. Stir occasionally to prevent sticking and ensure even cooking.
6. **Finish and Serve:**
   - Once the sukuma wiki is tender, season with salt and pepper to taste.
   - If desired, squeeze lemon or lime juice over the dish for a tangy flavor.
7. **Serve:**

- Serve Kenyan Sukuma Wiki hot, as a side dish with ugali (maize meal porridge), rice, or any other main dish of your choice.

Kenyan Sukuma Wiki is a simple yet flavorful dish that highlights the freshness of collard greens and the aromatic blend of spices and aromatics. It's a nutritious addition to any meal and is enjoyed across Kenya for its hearty and comforting qualities.

Algerian Chorba

Ingredients:

- 250g lamb or beef, cut into small cubes
- 2 tablespoons vegetable oil
- 1 large onion, finely chopped
- 2 cloves garlic, minced
- 2 tomatoes, chopped
- 1 tablespoon tomato paste
- 1 teaspoon ground turmeric
- 1 teaspoon ground cumin
- 1 teaspoon paprika
- 1/2 teaspoon ground cinnamon
- 1/4 teaspoon ground ginger
- 1/4 teaspoon ground cloves
- 1/4 teaspoon ground nutmeg
- Salt and pepper to taste
- 1 liter (4 cups) beef or chicken broth
- 1 liter (4 cups) water
- 1/2 cup dried chickpeas, soaked overnight (or canned chickpeas, drained and rinsed)
- 1/2 cup vermicelli or broken angel hair pasta
- Juice of 1/2 lemon
- Fresh cilantro or parsley, chopped, for garnish
- Lemon wedges, for serving

Instructions:

1. **Prepare the Meat:**
    - In a large pot, heat the vegetable oil over medium-high heat. Add the chopped onion and minced garlic. Sauté until softened and translucent, about 5 minutes.
    - Add the chopped tomatoes and tomato paste. Cook for another 5-7 minutes until the tomatoes break down and release their juices.
2. **Add Spices:**
    - Stir in the ground turmeric, cumin, paprika, cinnamon, ginger, cloves, nutmeg, salt, and pepper. Cook for 1-2 minutes until the spices are fragrant.
3. **Cook the Meat:**
    - Add the cubed lamb or beef to the pot. Brown the meat on all sides, stirring occasionally, for about 5-7 minutes.
4. **Simmer the Soup:**
    - Pour in the beef or chicken broth and water. Bring the mixture to a boil, then reduce the heat to low. Cover the pot and let it simmer gently for 1-1.5 hours, or until the meat is tender.

- If using dried chickpeas, add them to the pot during the last 30-45 minutes of cooking. If using canned chickpeas, add them towards the end of cooking.

5. **Add Vermicelli or Pasta:**
    - Once the meat and chickpeas are tender, add the vermicelli or broken angel hair pasta to the pot. Cook until the pasta is al dente, about 7-10 minutes.
6. **Finish and Serve:**
    - Stir in the lemon juice to brighten the flavors.
    - Taste and adjust seasoning if needed.
    - Serve Algerian Chorba hot, garnished with chopped fresh cilantro or parsley.
    - Serve with lemon wedges on the side for squeezing over the soup.

Algerian Chorba is a hearty and satisfying soup that brings together a rich blend of spices with tender meat and vegetables. It's perfect for warming up on a chilly day and is often enjoyed with crusty bread or alongside other Algerian dishes.

Senegalese Thieboudienne (Fish and Rice)

Ingredients:

For the Marinade:

- 4-6 pieces of fish (such as tilapia, red snapper, or grouper)
- Juice of 1 lemon
- Salt and pepper

For the Sauce (Sauce Rouge):

- 2 tablespoons vegetable oil
- 1 onion, finely chopped
- 3 cloves garlic, minced
- 2 tablespoons tomato paste
- 2 large tomatoes, chopped
- 1 teaspoon ground red pepper (cayenne pepper), or to taste
- 1 teaspoon ground black pepper
- 1 teaspoon ground mustard seeds
- 1 teaspoon ground ginger
- 1 teaspoon ground thyme
- 1 teaspoon ground cloves
- 2 bay leaves
- 2 cups water or fish stock
- Salt to taste

For the Thieb (Rice and Vegetables):

- 2 cups rice (preferably broken jasmine rice or similar)
- 1 large carrot, peeled and sliced into rounds
- 1 large sweet potato, peeled and cut into chunks
- 1 large eggplant, sliced into rounds
- 1/2 cabbage, cut into wedges
- 1-2 habanero peppers (optional, for heat)
- Salt to taste

For Garnish:

- Fresh parsley or cilantro, chopped

Instructions:

1. **Marinate the Fish:**

- Place the fish pieces in a bowl and squeeze lemon juice over them. Season with salt and pepper. Let marinate while you prepare the other ingredients.
2. **Prepare the Sauce (Sauce Rouge):**
    - Heat vegetable oil in a large, heavy-bottomed pot over medium heat.
    - Add chopped onion and minced garlic. Sauté until softened and translucent, about 5 minutes.
    - Stir in tomato paste and cook for 2-3 minutes until it darkens in color.
    - Add chopped tomatoes, ground red pepper, black pepper, mustard seeds, ginger, thyme, cloves, and bay leaves. Stir well to combine.
    - Pour in water or fish stock. Bring to a simmer and cook for 15-20 minutes, stirring occasionally, until the sauce thickens and flavors meld together. Adjust seasoning with salt to taste.
3. **Prepare the Thieb (Rice and Vegetables):**
    - Rinse the rice under cold water until the water runs clear. Drain and set aside.
    - Arrange the sliced vegetables (carrot, sweet potato, eggplant, cabbage) and habanero peppers (if using) over the sauce in the pot.
    - Place the marinated fish pieces on top of the vegetables. Pour any remaining marinade over the fish.
    - Add the rice evenly over the fish and vegetables.
4. **Cook the Thieboudienne:**
    - Pour enough water into the pot to just cover the rice and vegetables.
    - Bring the pot to a boil, then reduce the heat to low. Cover and simmer gently for 30-40 minutes, or until the rice is cooked and the fish and vegetables are tender. Avoid stirring to prevent the rice from becoming mushy; instead, gently shake the pot occasionally to redistribute the ingredients.
5. **Serve:**
    - Remove the bay leaves and habanero peppers (if used).
    - Serve Senegalese Thieboudienne hot, garnished with fresh parsley or cilantro.

Thieboudienne is a delightful dish that brings together the flavors of West Africa in a harmonious blend of fish, vegetables, and spices. It's a wonderful representation of Senegalese culinary traditions and is enjoyed as a communal meal shared with family and friends.

Tunisian Chickpea Stew

Ingredients:

- 2 cups cooked chickpeas (or 1 can, drained and rinsed)
- 4 cups vegetable broth or water
- 4 cloves garlic, minced
- 1 tablespoon olive oil
- 1 teaspoon ground cumin
- 1 teaspoon ground coriander
- 1 teaspoon paprika
- 1/2 teaspoon ground turmeric
- 1/4 teaspoon cayenne pepper (adjust to taste)
- Salt and pepper to taste
- Juice of 1 lemon
- Crusty bread, for serving
- Hard-boiled eggs (optional), for serving
- Fresh parsley or cilantro, chopped, for garnish

Optional toppings:

- Sliced red onion
- Capers
- Olives
- Harissa paste

Instructions:

1. **Prepare the Chickpeas:**
    - If using dried chickpeas, soak them overnight in water. Rinse and drain before using. Alternatively, use canned chickpeas, drained and rinsed.
2. **Sauté Garlic and Spices:**
    - Heat olive oil in a large pot over medium heat. Add minced garlic and sauté for 1-2 minutes until fragrant.
    - Add ground cumin, ground coriander, paprika, ground turmeric, and cayenne pepper. Stir for another minute until spices are toasted and fragrant.
3. **Cook the Stew:**
    - Add the cooked chickpeas to the pot, stirring to coat them with the spices.
    - Pour in vegetable broth or water. Bring the mixture to a simmer.
    - Reduce the heat to low and let the stew simmer gently for about 20-30 minutes, stirring occasionally, until the flavors meld together and the stew thickens slightly.
4. **Season and Serve:**
    - Season the stew with salt and pepper to taste.
    - Stir in the lemon juice for brightness and acidity.

5. **Serve:**
    - Ladle Tunisian Chickpea Stew into bowls.
    - Serve hot, garnished with chopped fresh parsley or cilantro.
    - Optionally, serve with crusty bread for dipping and hard-boiled eggs, sliced red onion, capers, olives, or a dollop of harissa paste on the side for additional flavor and texture.

Tunisian Chickpea Stew (Lablabi) is a delicious and nutritious dish that's perfect for any time of day. It's versatile, comforting, and showcases the vibrant flavors of North African cuisine. Enjoy it as a hearty meal on its own or as part of a larger spread with other Tunisian dishes.

Malawian Nsima with Beef Stew

Ingredients:

- 2 cups maize flour (white cornmeal or semolina can be used as substitutes)
- 4-5 cups water
- Salt to taste

Instructions:

1. **Boil Water:**
   - In a large, heavy-bottomed pot, bring 4 cups of water to a boil over medium-high heat.
2. **Add Maize Flour:**
   - Gradually add the maize flour to the boiling water, stirring constantly with a wooden spoon or whisk to prevent lumps from forming.
3. **Stir Continuously:**
   - Continue stirring vigorously until the mixture thickens and starts to pull away from the sides of the pot. This process takes about 10-15 minutes.
4. **Adjust Consistency:**
   - If the porridge is too thick, gradually add more water (up to 1 cup) and continue stirring until desired consistency is reached. It should be smooth and stiff enough to hold its shape.
5. **Season with Salt:**
   - Add salt to taste, stirring well to incorporate.
6. **Serve:**
   - Remove from heat and let it rest for a few minutes before serving. Nsima is traditionally shaped into a ball or oval and served with the stew.

Beef Stew:

Ingredients:

- 500g beef stew meat, cubed
- 2 tablespoons vegetable oil
- 1 onion, finely chopped
- 2 tomatoes, chopped
- 3 cloves garlic, minced
- 1 tablespoon tomato paste
- 1 teaspoon paprika
- 1 teaspoon ground cumin
- 1 teaspoon ground coriander
- 1/2 teaspoon ground cinnamon
- 1/2 teaspoon ground cloves
- Salt and pepper to taste

- 2 cups beef broth or water
- Fresh cilantro or parsley, chopped, for garnish

Instructions:

1. **Brown the Beef:**
    - Heat vegetable oil in a large pot or Dutch oven over medium-high heat. Add the cubed beef and brown on all sides, working in batches if necessary. Remove the beef and set aside.
2. **Sauté Aromatics:**
    - In the same pot, add chopped onion and sauté until softened and translucent, about 5 minutes.
    - Add minced garlic and sauté for another minute until fragrant.
3. **Add Tomatoes and Spices:**
    - Stir in chopped tomatoes and tomato paste. Cook for 5-7 minutes until tomatoes break down and release their juices.
    - Add paprika, ground cumin, ground coriander, ground cinnamon, and ground cloves. Stir well to combine.
4. **Simmer the Stew:**
    - Return the browned beef to the pot. Pour in beef broth or water, enough to cover the beef. Bring to a boil, then reduce the heat to low. Cover and simmer gently for 1.5 to 2 hours, or until the beef is tender and the sauce has thickened.
5. **Adjust Seasoning and Serve:**
    - Taste and adjust seasoning with salt and pepper as needed.
    - Serve Malawian Nsima hot, accompanied by the beef stew. Garnish with chopped fresh cilantro or parsley.

Serving:

- To serve, scoop a portion of Nsima onto a plate or bowl and create a well in the center. Ladle some beef stew into the well and garnish with fresh herbs.
- Nsima is traditionally eaten with your hands, using it to scoop up the stew. Enjoy the rich flavors and hearty textures of this traditional Malawian dish!

This meal is not only delicious but also reflects the cultural and culinary traditions of Malawi, showcasing the importance of maize and beef in the local diet.

Cameroonian Ndolé (Bitterleaf Stew)

Ingredients:

For the Ndolé:

- 500g (about 1 lb) bitterleaf greens (can substitute with spinach or kale, if bitterleaf is unavailable)
- 500g beef or pork, cut into bite-sized pieces (can also use chicken or fish)
- 1 cup raw peanuts, shelled
- 1 onion, finely chopped
- 3 cloves garlic, minced
- 1 tablespoon fresh ginger, grated
- 2 tablespoons vegetable oil
- 2 cups beef or chicken broth
- 1 cup water
- 1 tablespoon tomato paste
- Salt and pepper to taste
- 1 teaspoon ground crayfish (optional, for additional flavor)
- 1-2 Scotch bonnet or habanero peppers, whole (optional, for heat)
- 1/2 cup dried shrimp (optional, for additional flavor)

For the Peanut Paste (Pâte d'arachide):

- 1 cup raw peanuts, shelled
- Water

Instructions:

1. Prepare the Peanut Paste (Pâte d'arachide):

- Roast the raw peanuts in a dry skillet over medium heat until they are lightly browned and aromatic, about 5-7 minutes. Stir frequently to prevent burning.
- Remove the peanuts from the heat and let them cool slightly. Rub them between your hands or use a clean kitchen towel to remove the skins.
- Grind the roasted peanuts in a food processor or blender until they form a smooth paste, adding a little water gradually to help with blending. The paste should be thick and creamy. Set aside.

2. Prepare the Bitterleaf Greens:

- If using bitterleaf greens, wash them thoroughly to remove bitterness. This can be done by soaking them in salted water for about 10-15 minutes, then rinsing well. Alternatively, blanch them in boiling water for a few minutes, then drain and rinse.
- Chop the bitterleaf greens finely and set aside.

3. Cook the Meat:

- In a large pot or Dutch oven, heat vegetable oil over medium-high heat. Add chopped onion and sauté until softened, about 5 minutes.
- Add minced garlic and grated ginger, and cook for another 1-2 minutes until fragrant.
- Add the beef or pork pieces to the pot and brown them on all sides.

4. Prepare the Ndolé:

- Add tomato paste to the pot and stir well to coat the meat.
- Pour in beef or chicken broth and water. Bring to a boil, then reduce the heat to low.
- Stir in the peanut paste (Pâte d'arachide) and ground crayfish (if using). Mix well to combine and simmer gently for about 30 minutes, stirring occasionally, until the meat is tender and the stew thickens.
- If using dried shrimp and Scotch bonnet peppers, add them to the pot at this point for additional flavor. Adjust seasoning with salt and pepper to taste.

5. Add the Bitterleaf Greens:

- Add the chopped bitterleaf greens to the pot. Stir well to combine with the stew.
- Simmer the Ndolé for another 10-15 minutes, or until the bitterleaf greens are tender and cooked through.

6. Serve:

- Remove Scotch bonnet peppers if used whole before serving.
- Serve Cameroonian Ndolé hot, traditionally with rice or boiled plantains.

Enjoy the rich and nutty flavors of Cameroonian Ndolé, a dish that reflects the diverse culinary traditions of Cameroon and the Central African region!

Libyan Shorba (Lamb and Vegetable Stew)

Ingredients:

- 500g lamb shoulder or leg, cut into cubes
- 2 tablespoons vegetable oil
- 1 onion, finely chopped
- 3 cloves garlic, minced
- 2 tomatoes, chopped
- 1 tablespoon tomato paste
- 1 teaspoon ground cumin
- 1 teaspoon ground coriander
- 1/2 teaspoon ground turmeric
- 1/2 teaspoon ground cinnamon
- 1/4 teaspoon ground cloves
- Salt and pepper to taste
- 1 liter (4 cups) beef or lamb broth
- 2 cups water
- 1 large carrot, peeled and diced
- 1 large potato, peeled and diced
- 1 zucchini, diced
- 1/2 cup dried lentils, rinsed
- 1/2 cup chopped fresh cilantro or parsley, plus more for garnish
- Juice of 1/2 lemon

Instructions:

1. **Brown the Lamb:**
   - Heat vegetable oil in a large pot or Dutch oven over medium-high heat.
   - Add the lamb cubes and brown them on all sides. This will take about 5-7 minutes. Remove the lamb from the pot and set aside.
2. **Sauté Aromatics:**
   - In the same pot, add the chopped onion and sauté until softened, about 5 minutes.
   - Add minced garlic and sauté for another minute until fragrant.
3. **Add Tomatoes and Spices:**
   - Stir in chopped tomatoes and tomato paste. Cook for about 5 minutes until tomatoes are softened and begin to break down.
4. **Simmer the Stew:**
   - Return the browned lamb to the pot. Add ground cumin, ground coriander, ground turmeric, ground cinnamon, ground cloves, salt, and pepper. Stir well to coat the lamb with the spices.

- Pour in beef or lamb broth and water. Bring the mixture to a boil, then reduce the heat to low. Cover the pot and let it simmer gently for about 1 hour, stirring occasionally.

5. **Add Vegetables and Lentils:**
    - After 1 hour of simmering, add diced carrot, potato, zucchini, and rinsed lentils to the pot. Stir to combine.
    - Continue to simmer, partially covered, for another 30-40 minutes or until the lamb is tender, vegetables are cooked through, and lentils are tender.
6. **Finish and Serve:**
    - Stir in chopped fresh cilantro or parsley and lemon juice. Adjust seasoning with salt and pepper if needed.
    - Remove from heat and let the flavors meld for a few minutes.
7. **Serve:**
    - Ladle Libyan Shorba into bowls.
    - Garnish with additional chopped fresh cilantro or parsley.

Enjoy Libyan Shorba hot, accompanied by crusty bread or rice. This stew is not only delicious but also a comforting and nourishing meal that showcases the rich flavors of Libyan cuisine.

Zimbabwean Peanut Butter Stew

Ingredients:

- 500g chicken thighs or beef stew meat, cut into bite-sized pieces
- 2 tablespoons vegetable oil
- 1 onion, finely chopped
- 3 cloves garlic, minced
- 1 tablespoon fresh ginger, grated
- 2 tomatoes, chopped
- 1 tablespoon tomato paste
- 1 cup natural peanut butter (unsweetened)
- 1 teaspoon ground coriander
- 1 teaspoon ground cumin
- 1/2 teaspoon ground cinnamon
- 1/2 teaspoon paprika
- 1/4 teaspoon cayenne pepper (adjust to taste)
- Salt and pepper to taste
- 4 cups chicken or beef broth
- 2 cups water
- 2 cups butternut squash, peeled and diced (or sweet potatoes)
- 1 cup okra, trimmed and sliced (optional)
- Juice of 1/2 lemon or lime
- Fresh cilantro or parsley, chopped, for garnish

Instructions:

1. **Brown the Meat:**
   - Heat vegetable oil in a large pot or Dutch oven over medium-high heat.
   - Add the chicken thighs or beef pieces and brown them on all sides. Remove from the pot and set aside.
2. **Sauté Aromatics:**
   - In the same pot, add chopped onion and sauté until softened and translucent, about 5 minutes.
   - Add minced garlic and grated ginger. Sauté for another 1-2 minutes until fragrant.
3. **Add Tomatoes and Spices:**
   - Stir in chopped tomatoes and tomato paste. Cook for 5-7 minutes until tomatoes break down and release their juices.
   - Add ground coriander, ground cumin, ground cinnamon, paprika, cayenne pepper, salt, and pepper. Stir well to combine with the aromatics.
4. **Make the Peanut Butter Mixture:**
   - In a bowl, whisk together the peanut butter with a cup of warm water until smooth and well combined. Add more water if needed to achieve a pourable consistency.
5. **Cook the Stew:**

- Return the browned meat to the pot. Pour in chicken or beef broth and water.
- Add diced butternut squash (or sweet potatoes) and sliced okra (if using).
- Pour in the peanut butter mixture, stirring well to combine all ingredients.
- Bring the stew to a boil, then reduce the heat to low. Cover and let it simmer gently for about 45-60 minutes, or until the meat is tender and the vegetables are cooked through. Stir occasionally to prevent sticking.

6. **Finish and Serve:**
    - Stir in the juice of half a lemon or lime to brighten the flavors.
    - Taste and adjust seasoning with salt and pepper if needed.
    - Serve Zimbabwean Peanut Butter Stew hot, garnished with chopped fresh cilantro or parsley.

Enjoy this delicious and hearty Zimbabwean Peanut Butter Stew with sadza (maize porridge) or rice. The creamy peanut butter base combined with savory spices creates a unique and satisfying dish that is sure to be a hit at any meal!

Ivorian Kedjenou (Chicken Stew)

Ingredients:

- 1 whole chicken (about 1.5 kg), cut into pieces
- 2 onions, finely chopped
- 3 tomatoes, chopped
- 2 bell peppers (1 red, 1 green), sliced
- 2-3 hot peppers (habanero or Scotch bonnet), whole (optional, for heat)
- 4 cloves garlic, minced
- 2 inches fresh ginger, grated
- 2 tablespoons vegetable oil
- 2 tablespoons tomato paste
- 1 teaspoon paprika
- 1 teaspoon ground cumin
- 1 teaspoon ground coriander
- 1/2 teaspoon ground cloves
- 1/2 teaspoon ground nutmeg
- 2 bay leaves
- Salt and pepper to taste
- 1/2 cup water or chicken broth
- Fresh parsley or cilantro, chopped, for garnish

Instructions:

1. **Prepare the Chicken:**
   - Clean and cut the chicken into pieces. If using skin-on chicken, you can remove the skin or leave it on based on your preference.
2. **Marinate the Chicken:**
   - In a large bowl, combine the chicken pieces with minced garlic, grated ginger, paprika, ground cumin, ground coriander, ground cloves, ground nutmeg, salt, and pepper. Mix well to coat the chicken evenly. Let it marinate for at least 30 minutes, or preferably overnight in the refrigerator.
3. **Sauté Aromatics:**
   - Heat vegetable oil in a large, heavy-bottomed pot or Dutch oven over medium-high heat.
   - Add chopped onions and sauté until softened and translucent, about 5-7 minutes.
4. **Add Tomatoes and Peppers:**
   - Add chopped tomatoes, sliced bell peppers, and whole hot peppers (if using) to the pot. Cook for another 5 minutes until the tomatoes start to break down.
5. **Cook the Chicken:**
   - Add the marinated chicken pieces to the pot, along with bay leaves. Stir well to combine with the vegetables.

- Cook the chicken for about 10 minutes, stirring occasionally, until it starts to brown slightly.
6. **Simmer the Stew:**
    - Reduce the heat to low. Dissolve tomato paste in water or chicken broth and pour it over the chicken and vegetables.
    - Cover the pot tightly with a lid (or use aluminum foil to seal the pot) to create a tight seal. This method helps to steam and cook the chicken in its own juices.
    - Let the Kedjenou simmer gently for about 1 to 1.5 hours, or until the chicken is tender and cooked through. Stir occasionally to prevent sticking and check for doneness.
7. **Finish and Serve:**
    - Taste and adjust seasoning with salt and pepper if needed.
    - Garnish Ivorian Kedjenou with chopped fresh parsley or cilantro before serving.
8. **Serve:**
    - Serve Ivorian Kedjenou hot, traditionally with steamed rice or boiled yams.

Enjoy the fragrant and tender Ivorian Kedjenou, a dish that captures the essence of Ivorian cuisine with its blend of spices and slow-cooked goodness!

Eritrean Zigni (Spicy Beef Stew)

Ingredients:

- 500g beef stew meat, cubed
- 2 tablespoons vegetable oil
- 2 onions, finely chopped
- 4 cloves garlic, minced
- 1 tablespoon fresh ginger, grated
- 2 tomatoes, chopped
- 2 tablespoons tomato paste
- 1 tablespoon berbere spice mix*
- 1 teaspoon ground cumin
- 1 teaspoon ground coriander
- 1/2 teaspoon ground cardamom
- 1/4 teaspoon ground cloves
- 1/4 teaspoon ground cinnamon
- 1/4 teaspoon ground nutmeg
- Salt to taste
- 2 cups water or beef broth
- 1-2 hot green chilies (optional, for extra heat)
- Fresh cilantro, chopped, for garnish

Instructions:

1. **Prepare the Beef:**
   - Heat vegetable oil in a large pot or Dutch oven over medium-high heat.
   - Add the cubed beef and brown on all sides. This will take about 5-7 minutes. Remove the beef from the pot and set aside.
2. **Sauté Aromatics:**
   - In the same pot, add chopped onions and sauté until softened and translucent, about 5-7 minutes.
   - Add minced garlic and grated ginger. Sauté for another 1-2 minutes until fragrant.
3. **Add Tomatoes and Spices:**
   - Stir in chopped tomatoes and tomato paste. Cook for about 5 minutes until tomatoes break down and release their juices.
   - Add berbere spice mix, ground cumin, ground coriander, ground cardamom, ground cloves, ground cinnamon, and ground nutmeg. Stir well to combine with the aromatics.
4. **Simmer the Stew:**
   - Return the browned beef to the pot. Pour in water or beef broth.
   - If using hot green chilies for extra heat, add them whole to the pot.

- Bring the mixture to a boil, then reduce the heat to low. Cover the pot and let it simmer gently for about 1.5 to 2 hours, or until the beef is tender and the stew has thickened. Stir occasionally.
5. **Finish and Serve:**
    - Taste and adjust seasoning with salt if needed.
    - Remove hot green chilies if used.
    - Serve Eritrean Zigni hot, garnished with chopped fresh cilantro.
6. **Serve:**
    - Eritrean Zigni is traditionally served with injera, a sourdough flatbread, for scooping up the stew. It can also be served with rice or crusty bread.

Enjoy the bold flavors and spices of Eritrean Zigni, a dish that reflects the vibrant culinary traditions of Eritrea!

Sierra Leonean Cassava Leaf Stew

Ingredients:

- 500g cassava leaves (fresh or frozen), chopped finely (if using fresh, ensure they are thoroughly washed and pounded or blended)
- 500g chicken, beef, or fish, cut into bite-sized pieces
- 2 tablespoons palm oil (substitute with vegetable oil if palm oil is unavailable)
- 1 onion, finely chopped
- 3 cloves garlic, minced
- 1 tablespoon fresh ginger, grated
- 2 tomatoes, chopped (or 1 cup tomato puree)
- 2 tablespoons tomato paste
- 1 Maggi cube or bouillon cube (optional, for additional flavor)
- 1 teaspoon ground cayenne pepper (adjust to taste)
- Salt to taste
- 4 cups water or chicken broth
- 1 cup peanut butter (natural, unsweetened)
- Fresh lemon or lime juice, to taste
- Cooked rice or fufu (for serving)

Instructions:

1. **Prepare the Cassava Leaves:**
   - If using fresh cassava leaves, ensure they are finely chopped, washed thoroughly, and pounded or blended to break down tough fibers.
2. **Cook the Meat:**
   - In a large pot or Dutch oven, heat palm oil over medium-high heat.
   - Add chopped onion and sauté until softened, about 5-7 minutes.
   - Add minced garlic and grated ginger. Sauté for another 1-2 minutes until fragrant.
   - Add chicken, beef, or fish pieces to the pot. Brown them on all sides, stirring occasionally.
3. **Add Tomatoes and Spices:**
   - Stir in chopped tomatoes (or tomato puree) and tomato paste. Cook for about 5 minutes until tomatoes break down and release their juices.
   - Add ground cayenne pepper, Maggi cube or bouillon cube (if using), and salt to taste. Stir well to combine.
4. **Simmer the Stew:**
   - Pour in water or chicken broth to the pot, enough to cover the meat and vegetables. Bring the mixture to a boil.
5. **Add Cassava Leaves and Peanut Butter:**
   - Add chopped cassava leaves to the pot. Stir well to combine with the meat and vegetables.

- Reduce the heat to low and let the stew simmer gently for about 1 to 1.5 hours, stirring occasionally. This allows the flavors to meld together and the cassava leaves to cook down.

6. **Incorporate Peanut Butter:**
    - Stir in peanut butter to the stew, mixing well until it is fully incorporated and the stew thickens slightly. Cook for an additional 10-15 minutes.
7. **Finish and Serve:**
    - Add fresh lemon or lime juice to taste, adjusting the acidity as desired.
    - Serve Sierra Leonean Cassava Leaf Stew hot, traditionally with cooked rice or fufu (a starchy side dish).

Enjoy the hearty and flavorful Sierra Leonean Cassava Leaf Stew, a dish that reflects the culinary diversity and richness of West African cuisine!

Moroccan Harira (Tomato and Lentil Soup)

Ingredients:

- 1 cup dried chickpeas, soaked overnight (or use canned chickpeas, drained and rinsed)
- 1/2 cup dried lentils, rinsed
- 2 tablespoons olive oil
- 1 onion, finely chopped
- 3 cloves garlic, minced
- 2 celery stalks, finely chopped
- 1 carrot, peeled and finely chopped
- 2 tomatoes, chopped (or 1 can of chopped tomatoes)
- 1 tablespoon tomato paste
- 1 teaspoon ground turmeric
- 1 teaspoon ground ginger
- 1 teaspoon ground cinnamon
- 1/2 teaspoon ground cumin
- 1/2 teaspoon ground coriander
- 1/4 teaspoon cayenne pepper (optional, for heat)
- Salt and pepper to taste
- 1 liter (4 cups) vegetable or chicken broth
- 1/4 cup fresh parsley, chopped
- 1/4 cup fresh cilantro, chopped
- Juice of 1 lemon
- 2 tablespoons all-purpose flour (optional, for thickening)
- 2 tablespoons water (optional, for thickening)
- Lemon wedges, for serving
- Hard-boiled eggs, chopped (optional, for garnish)

Instructions:

1. **Prepare Chickpeas and Lentils:**
    - If using dried chickpeas, soak them overnight in water. Drain and rinse before using.
    - Rinse dried lentils under cold water.
2. **Sauté Aromatics:**
    - Heat olive oil in a large pot over medium heat. Add chopped onion, garlic, celery, and carrot. Sauté until softened, about 5-7 minutes.
3. **Add Tomatoes and Spices:**
    - Stir in chopped tomatoes and tomato paste. Cook for about 5 minutes until tomatoes start to break down.
    - Add ground turmeric, ground ginger, ground cinnamon, ground cumin, ground coriander, cayenne pepper (if using), salt, and pepper. Stir well to combine with the vegetables.

4. **Simmer the Soup:**
   - Add soaked chickpeas (or canned chickpeas) and rinsed lentils to the pot.
   - Pour in vegetable or chicken broth. Bring the mixture to a boil, then reduce the heat to low. Cover the pot and let it simmer gently for about 45 minutes to 1 hour, or until chickpeas and lentils are tender.
5. **Thicken the Soup (Optional):**
   - In a small bowl, mix together flour and water to create a slurry. Stir the slurry into the soup to thicken it, if desired. Cook for an additional 5-10 minutes.
6. **Finish the Soup:**
   - Stir in chopped parsley, cilantro, and lemon juice. Taste and adjust seasoning with salt and pepper if needed.
   - If using, garnish Moroccan Harira with chopped hard-boiled eggs.
7. **Serve:**
   - Serve Moroccan Harira hot, garnished with additional fresh herbs and lemon wedges on the side.

Enjoy the comforting flavors of Moroccan Harira, a wholesome soup that is perfect for any occasion, particularly during Ramadan or as a nourishing meal throughout the year!

Somali Suqaar (Beef Stew)

Ingredients:

- 500g beef sirloin or stew meat, cut into small cubes
- 2 tablespoons vegetable oil
- 1 onion, finely chopped
- 3 cloves garlic, minced
- 1 tablespoon fresh ginger, grated
- 2 tomatoes, chopped
- 1 tablespoon tomato paste
- 1 teaspoon ground cumin
- 1 teaspoon ground coriander
- 1/2 teaspoon ground turmeric
- 1/2 teaspoon ground black pepper
- 1/4 teaspoon ground cinnamon
- 1/4 teaspoon ground cloves
- Salt to taste
- 1 green bell pepper, diced
- 1 red bell pepper, diced
- 1 jalapeño or green chili, finely chopped (optional, for heat)
- Fresh cilantro or parsley, chopped, for garnish
- Lemon wedges, for serving

Instructions:

1. **Prepare the Beef:**
    - Heat vegetable oil in a large skillet or frying pan over medium-high heat.
    - Add the beef cubes in batches and brown them on all sides. Remove the beef from the pan and set aside.
2. **Sauté Aromatics:**
    - In the same skillet, add chopped onion and sauté until softened and translucent, about 5-7 minutes.
    - Add minced garlic and grated ginger. Sauté for another 1-2 minutes until fragrant.
3. **Add Tomatoes and Spices:**
    - Stir in chopped tomatoes and tomato paste. Cook for about 5 minutes until tomatoes break down and release their juices.
    - Add ground cumin, ground coriander, ground turmeric, ground black pepper, ground cinnamon, ground cloves, and salt to taste. Stir well to combine with the aromatics.
4. **Cook the Beef:**
    - Return the browned beef cubes to the skillet. Mix well with the tomato and spice mixture.

- Reduce the heat to low, cover the skillet, and let it simmer gently for about 20-30 minutes, or until the beef is tender and cooked through. Stir occasionally to prevent sticking.

5. **Add Bell Peppers and Chili (Optional):**
    - Stir in diced green bell pepper, red bell pepper, and chopped jalapeño or green chili (if using). Cook for another 5-10 minutes until the vegetables are tender-crisp.
6. **Finish and Serve:**
    - Taste and adjust seasoning with salt and pepper if needed.
    - Garnish Somali Suqaar with chopped fresh cilantro or parsley.
    - Serve hot, accompanied by rice, bread, or Somali flatbread (like Anjero or Injera).
7. **Serve:**
    - Serve Somali Suqaar hot, garnished with fresh cilantro or parsley and lemon wedges on the side.

Enjoy the delicious flavors of Somali Suqaar, a comforting and aromatic beef stew that is perfect for sharing with family and friends!

Namibian Oxtail Stew

Ingredients:

- 1.5 kg oxtail pieces
- 2 tablespoons vegetable oil
- 2 onions, finely chopped
- 3 cloves garlic, minced
- 2 carrots, peeled and diced
- 2 celery stalks, diced
- 2 tomatoes, chopped
- 2 tablespoons tomato paste
- 1 tablespoon Worcestershire sauce
- 1 teaspoon paprika
- 1 teaspoon ground coriander
- 1/2 teaspoon ground cumin
- 1/2 teaspoon dried thyme
- 1 bay leaf
- Salt and pepper to taste
- 4 cups beef broth
- 1 cup red wine (optional)
- Fresh parsley, chopped, for garnish

Instructions:

1. **Prepare the Oxtail:**
   - Rinse the oxtail pieces under cold water and pat dry with paper towels.
2. **Brown the Oxtail:**
   - Heat vegetable oil in a large Dutch oven or heavy-bottomed pot over medium-high heat.
   - Working in batches, add the oxtail pieces and brown them on all sides. Remove from the pot and set aside.
3. **Sauté Aromatics:**
   - In the same pot, add chopped onions and sauté until softened, about 5 minutes.
   - Add minced garlic, diced carrots, and diced celery. Sauté for another 3-4 minutes until vegetables are slightly softened.
4. **Add Tomatoes and Seasonings:**
   - Stir in chopped tomatoes and tomato paste. Cook for about 5 minutes until tomatoes break down.
   - Add Worcestershire sauce, paprika, ground coriander, ground cumin, dried thyme, bay leaf, salt, and pepper. Stir well to combine with the vegetables.
5. **Simmer the Stew:**
   - Return the browned oxtail pieces to the pot.

- Pour in beef broth and red wine (if using), ensuring that the oxtail pieces are covered with liquid.
- Bring the mixture to a boil, then reduce the heat to low. Cover the pot and let it simmer gently for about 3-4 hours, or until the oxtail is tender and meat is falling off the bones. Stir occasionally and skim off any fat that rises to the surface.

6. **Finish and Serve:**
    - Taste and adjust seasoning with salt and pepper if needed.
    - Remove the bay leaf from the stew.
    - Garnish Namibian Oxtail Stew with chopped fresh parsley before serving.
7. **Serve:**
    - Serve Namibian Oxtail Stew hot, accompanied by rice, mashed potatoes, or crusty bread.

Enjoy the hearty and comforting flavors of Namibian Oxtail Stew, a dish that's perfect for warming up on chilly days and impressing guests with its rich taste!

Rwandan Chicken and Plantain Stew

Ingredients:

- 1 kg chicken pieces (legs, thighs, or bone-in breasts)
- 3 ripe plantains, peeled and cut into thick slices
- 2 tablespoons vegetable oil
- 1 onion, finely chopped
- 3 cloves garlic, minced
- 1 tablespoon fresh ginger, grated
- 2 tomatoes, chopped
- 1 tablespoon tomato paste
- 1 teaspoon ground coriander
- 1 teaspoon ground cumin
- 1/2 teaspoon ground turmeric
- 1/2 teaspoon ground cinnamon
- 1/4 teaspoon ground cloves
- 1/4 teaspoon cayenne pepper (adjust to taste)
- Salt and pepper to taste
- 4 cups chicken broth
- Fresh cilantro or parsley, chopped, for garnish

Instructions:

1. **Prepare the Chicken:**
   - Rinse the chicken pieces under cold water and pat dry with paper towels.
2. **Sauté the Chicken:**
   - Heat vegetable oil in a large pot or Dutch oven over medium-high heat.
   - Add the chicken pieces and brown them on all sides, working in batches if necessary. Remove from the pot and set aside.
3. **Sauté Aromatics:**
   - In the same pot, add chopped onion and sauté until softened, about 5-7 minutes.
   - Add minced garlic and grated ginger. Sauté for another 1-2 minutes until fragrant.
4. **Add Tomatoes and Spices:**
   - Stir in chopped tomatoes and tomato paste. Cook for about 5 minutes until tomatoes break down.
   - Add ground coriander, ground cumin, ground turmeric, ground cinnamon, ground cloves, cayenne pepper, salt, and pepper. Stir well to combine with the aromatics.
5. **Simmer the Stew:**
   - Return the browned chicken pieces to the pot.
   - Pour in chicken broth, ensuring that the chicken pieces are covered with liquid.
   - Bring the mixture to a boil, then reduce the heat to low. Cover the pot and let it simmer gently for about 30 minutes, stirring occasionally.
6. **Add Plantains:**

- After 30 minutes of simmering, add the sliced plantains to the pot. Stir gently to combine with the stew.
7. **Finish Cooking:**
    - Continue to simmer the stew for another 20-30 minutes, or until the chicken is tender and cooked through, and the plantains are softened.
8. **Adjust Seasoning and Serve:**
    - Taste and adjust seasoning with salt, pepper, and additional cayenne pepper if desired.
    - Garnish Rwandan Chicken and Plantain Stew with chopped fresh cilantro or parsley before serving.
9. **Serve:**
    - Serve hot, accompanied by steamed rice or Rwandan Ugali (a thick maize porridge).

Enjoy the comforting and aromatic flavors of Rwandan Chicken and Plantain Stew, a dish that highlights the delicious combination of chicken and sweet plantains!

Egyptian Molokhia Stew

Ingredients:

- 500g frozen or fresh molokhia leaves (if using fresh, wash and finely chop)
- 1 kg chicken pieces (such as thighs or breasts) or 500g beef/lamb, cut into cubes
- 2 onions, finely chopped
- 4 cloves garlic, minced
- 2 tomatoes, chopped
- 2 tablespoons vegetable oil or clarified butter (samneh)
- 1 tablespoon ground coriander
- 1 teaspoon ground cumin
- 1/2 teaspoon ground cinnamon
- 1/4 teaspoon ground cloves
- Salt and pepper to taste
- 2 liters (8 cups) chicken broth or water
- Juice of 1 lemon
- Cooked rice or Egyptian vermicelli rice, for serving

Instructions:

1. **Prepare the Meat:**
   - If using chicken, wash the pieces under cold water and pat dry with paper towels. If using beef or lamb, cut into cubes and set aside.
2. **Sauté the Meat and Aromatics:**
   - Heat vegetable oil or clarified butter in a large pot over medium-high heat.
   - Add chopped onions and sauté until softened and translucent, about 5-7 minutes.
   - Add minced garlic and sauté for another 1-2 minutes until fragrant.
3. **Cook the Meat:**
   - Add the chicken pieces or cubed beef/lamb to the pot. Brown them on all sides, stirring occasionally.
4. **Add Tomatoes and Spices:**
   - Stir in chopped tomatoes, ground coriander, ground cumin, ground cinnamon, ground cloves, salt, and pepper. Cook for about 5 minutes until tomatoes break down and release their juices.
5. **Simmer the Stew:**
   - Pour in chicken broth or water, enough to cover the meat. Bring the mixture to a boil.
6. **Add Molokhia Leaves:**
   - Add the frozen or chopped fresh molokhia leaves to the pot. Stir well to combine with the meat and spices.
7. **Cook Molokhia Stew:**

- Reduce the heat to low and let the stew simmer gently for about 30-45 minutes, stirring occasionally. The molokhia leaves should cook down and thicken the stew.

8. **Finish and Serve:**
   - Stir in lemon juice to taste, adjusting the acidity as desired.
   - Taste and adjust seasoning with salt and pepper if needed.
9. **Serve:**
   - Serve Egyptian Molokhia Stew hot, traditionally over cooked rice or Egyptian vermicelli rice.

Enjoy the rich flavors and nutritious benefits of Egyptian Molokhia Stew, a comforting dish that is popular throughout the Middle East and North Africa!

Sudanese Bamia (Okra Stew)

Ingredients:

- 500g okra, washed, trimmed, and cut into rounds
- 500g beef stew meat, cut into cubes (you can also use lamb or chicken)
- 2 tablespoons vegetable oil
- 1 onion, finely chopped
- 3 cloves garlic, minced
- 2 tomatoes, chopped
- 1 tablespoon tomato paste
- 1 teaspoon ground coriander
- 1 teaspoon ground cumin
- 1/2 teaspoon ground turmeric
- 1/2 teaspoon ground paprika
- 1/4 teaspoon ground cinnamon
- 1/4 teaspoon ground cloves
- Salt and pepper to taste
- 4 cups beef or vegetable broth
- Juice of 1 lemon
- Fresh cilantro or parsley, chopped, for garnish
- Cooked rice or bread, for serving

Instructions:

1. **Prepare the Okra:**
    - Wash the okra pods under cold water. Trim off the tops and cut them into rounds. Set aside.
2. **Sauté the Meat:**
    - Heat vegetable oil in a large pot or Dutch oven over medium-high heat.
    - Add the cubed beef stew meat and brown on all sides. Remove from the pot and set aside.
3. **Sauté Aromatics:**
    - In the same pot, add chopped onion and sauté until softened and translucent, about 5 minutes.
    - Add minced garlic and sauté for another 1-2 minutes until fragrant.
4. **Add Tomatoes and Spices:**
    - Stir in chopped tomatoes and tomato paste. Cook for about 5 minutes until tomatoes break down and release their juices.
    - Add ground coriander, ground cumin, ground turmeric, ground paprika, ground cinnamon, ground cloves, salt, and pepper. Stir well to combine with the aromatics.
5. **Simmer the Stew:**
    - Return the browned meat to the pot.

- Pour in beef or vegetable broth, enough to cover the meat and vegetables. Bring the mixture to a boil.

6. **Add Okra:**
   - Add the sliced okra rounds to the pot. Stir gently to combine with the meat and spices.
7. **Cook Bamia Stew:**
   - Reduce the heat to low and let the stew simmer gently for about 30-40 minutes, or until the meat is tender and the okra is cooked through. Stir occasionally.
8. **Finish and Serve:**
   - Stir in lemon juice to taste, adjusting the acidity as desired.
   - Taste and adjust seasoning with salt and pepper if needed.
   - Garnish Sudanese Bamia with chopped fresh cilantro or parsley before serving.
9. **Serve:**
   - Serve Sudanese Bamia hot, accompanied by cooked rice or bread.

Enjoy the flavorful and aromatic Sudanese Bamia (Okra Stew), a dish that highlights the delicious combination of okra, meat, and spices, perfect for sharing with family and friends!

Beninese Gbegiri (Bean Soup)

Ingredients:

- 1 cup black-eyed peas or brown beans, dried
- 1 onion, chopped
- 2-3 cloves garlic, minced
- 2 tomatoes, chopped
- 2 tablespoons vegetable oil
- 1 teaspoon ground crayfish (optional, but traditional)
- 1 teaspoon ground cayenne pepper (adjust to taste)
- Salt to taste
- 4 cups water or vegetable broth
- Fresh parsley or cilantro, chopped, for garnish
- Cooked rice, for serving

Instructions:

1. **Prepare the Beans:**
   - Rinse the black-eyed peas or brown beans under cold water and soak them overnight in plenty of water. Alternatively, use the quick-soak method by bringing them to a boil in water for 2 minutes, then letting them sit for 1 hour off the heat. Drain and rinse.
2. **Cook the Beans:**
   - In a large pot, add the soaked and drained beans. Cover with water or vegetable broth (about 4 cups) and bring to a boil.
   - Reduce the heat to medium-low and simmer until the beans are tender, about 45 minutes to 1 hour. Skim off any foam that forms on the surface.
3. **Prepare the Base:**
   - In a separate pan, heat vegetable oil over medium heat. Add chopped onion and sauté until softened, about 5-7 minutes.
   - Add minced garlic and sauté for another 1-2 minutes until fragrant.
4. **Blend and Combine:**
   - Once the beans are tender, remove about half of them from the pot and blend them until smooth using a blender or food processor. Return the blended beans to the pot.
5. **Add Tomatoes and Spices:**
   - Add chopped tomatoes to the pot of beans. Stir well to combine.
   - Add ground crayfish (if using), ground cayenne pepper, and salt to taste. Stir well to incorporate all the flavors.
6. **Simmer the Soup:**
   - Simmer the Gbegiri soup over low heat for another 15-20 minutes, stirring occasionally, to allow the flavors to meld together and the soup to thicken slightly.
7. **Finish and Serve:**

- Taste and adjust seasoning with more salt or cayenne pepper if needed.
- Garnish Beninese Gbegiri with chopped fresh parsley or cilantro before serving.
- Serve hot with cooked rice on the side.

Enjoy the rich and flavorful Beninese Gbegiri soup, a comforting dish that showcases the hearty and nutritious qualities of beans, perfect for a wholesome meal!

Cape Verdean Catchupa (Corn Stew)

Ingredients:

- 1 cup dried hominy corn (or use canned hominy, drained and rinsed)
- 1 cup dried kidney beans (or use canned kidney beans, drained and rinsed)
- 250g pork belly or chorizo sausage, diced
- 250g beef or chicken, diced
- 1 onion, finely chopped
- 3 cloves garlic, minced
- 2 tomatoes, chopped
- 1 tablespoon tomato paste
- 2 tablespoons olive oil
- 1 bay leaf
- 1 teaspoon paprika
- 1/2 teaspoon ground cumin
- Salt and pepper to taste
- Water or beef/chicken broth (enough to cover)
- Chopped fresh parsley or cilantro, for garnish
- Hot sauce or piri piri sauce (optional), for serving

Instructions:

1. **Prepare the Hominy Corn and Beans:**
   - If using dried hominy corn and kidney beans, soak them separately in water overnight. Drain and rinse before cooking.
   - In separate pots, cook the hominy corn and kidney beans in water until tender. This may take 1-2 hours for the hominy corn and about 1 hour for the kidney beans. Alternatively, you can use canned hominy and kidney beans, which reduces cooking time significantly.
2. **Sauté the Meats:**
   - In a large pot or Dutch oven, heat olive oil over medium-high heat.
   - Add diced pork belly or chorizo sausage and diced beef or chicken. Sauté until browned on all sides.
3. **Sauté Aromatics:**
   - Add chopped onion and minced garlic to the pot with the meats. Sauté until the onion is softened, about 5 minutes.
4. **Add Tomatoes and Spices:**
   - Stir in chopped tomatoes and tomato paste. Cook for another 5 minutes until tomatoes break down and release their juices.
   - Add paprika, ground cumin, bay leaf, salt, and pepper. Stir well to combine with the aromatics.
5. **Combine Ingredients:**

- Add the cooked hominy corn and kidney beans to the pot with the meats and aromatics. Mix well to combine all the ingredients.
6. **Simmer the Catchupa:**
    - Pour enough water or beef/chicken broth into the pot to cover all the ingredients. Bring the mixture to a boil, then reduce the heat to low.
    - Let the Catchupa simmer gently for about 1-2 hours, stirring occasionally, until the flavors meld together and the stew thickens. Add more water or broth if needed to achieve your desired consistency.
7. **Finish and Serve:**
    - Taste and adjust seasoning with salt and pepper if needed.
    - Garnish Cape Verdean Catchupa with chopped fresh parsley or cilantro before serving.
    - Serve hot, optionally with hot sauce or piri piri sauce on the side for added spice.

Enjoy the comforting and flavorful Cape Verdean Catchupa, a dish that reflects the rich culinary traditions of Cape Verde!

Gabonese Poulet Nyembwe (Chicken in Palm Nut Sauce)

Ingredients:

- 1 whole chicken, cut into pieces (or use chicken thighs and drumsticks)
- 2 cups palm nut pulp (also known as palm nut cream or oil)
- 1 onion, finely chopped
- 2 tomatoes, chopped
- 3 cloves garlic, minced
- 1 tablespoon tomato paste
- 2 tablespoons vegetable oil
- 1 teaspoon ground ginger
- 1 teaspoon ground coriander
- 1/2 teaspoon ground black pepper
- 1/2 teaspoon ground nutmeg
- Salt to taste
- 2 cups chicken broth or water
- Fresh parsley or cilantro, chopped, for garnish
- Cooked rice or plantains, for serving

Instructions:

1. **Prepare the Chicken:**
    - Rinse the chicken pieces under cold water and pat dry with paper towels. Season with salt and pepper.
2. **Sauté the Chicken:**
    - Heat vegetable oil in a large pot or Dutch oven over medium-high heat.
    - Add the chicken pieces and brown them on all sides. Remove from the pot and set aside.
3. **Sauté Aromatics:**
    - In the same pot, add chopped onion and sauté until softened and translucent, about 5 minutes.
    - Add minced garlic and sauté for another 1-2 minutes until fragrant.
4. **Add Tomatoes and Tomato Paste:**
    - Stir in chopped tomatoes and tomato paste. Cook for about 5 minutes until tomatoes break down and release their juices.
5. **Prepare Palm Nut Sauce:**
    - Add palm nut pulp (or cream) to the pot. Stir well to combine with the aromatics.
6. **Season and Simmer:**
    - Add ground ginger, ground coriander, ground black pepper, ground nutmeg, and salt to taste. Mix well.
7. **Cook the Chicken in Palm Nut Sauce:**
    - Return the browned chicken pieces to the pot, along with any juices.
    - Pour in chicken broth or water, enough to cover the chicken pieces.

- Bring the mixture to a boil, then reduce the heat to low. Cover the pot and let it simmer gently for about 45 minutes to 1 hour, or until the chicken is tender and cooked through.

8. **Finish and Serve:**
    - Taste and adjust seasoning with salt and pepper if needed.
    - Garnish Gabonese Poulet Nyembwe with chopped fresh parsley or cilantro before serving.
    - Serve hot, accompanied by cooked rice or plantains.

Enjoy the rich and creamy flavors of Gabonese Poulet Nyembwe, a delightful dish that brings a taste of Gabonese cuisine to your table!

Burkina Faso's Riz Gras (Rice with Meat and Vegetables)

Ingredients:

- 2 cups long-grain white rice
- 500g beef or lamb, cut into cubes (you can also use chicken or pork)
- 2 tablespoons vegetable oil or clarified butter (samneh)
- 1 onion, finely chopped
- 3 cloves garlic, minced
- 2 tomatoes, chopped
- 1 tablespoon tomato paste
- 2 carrots, peeled and diced
- 1 green bell pepper, diced
- 1 cup green beans, trimmed and chopped
- 1 teaspoon ground ginger
- 1 teaspoon ground coriander
- 1/2 teaspoon ground cinnamon
- 1/4 teaspoon ground cloves
- 1/4 teaspoon ground nutmeg
- Salt and pepper to taste
- 4 cups beef or chicken broth
- Fresh parsley or cilantro, chopped, for garnish

Instructions:

1. **Prepare the Rice:**
   - Rinse the rice under cold water until the water runs clear. Drain and set aside.
2. **Cook the Meat:**
   - In a large pot or Dutch oven, heat vegetable oil or clarified butter over medium-high heat.
   - Add the cubed beef or lamb and brown on all sides. Remove from the pot and set aside.
3. **Sauté Aromatics:**
   - In the same pot, add chopped onion and sauté until softened and translucent, about 5-7 minutes.
   - Add minced garlic and sauté for another 1-2 minutes until fragrant.
4. **Add Tomatoes and Tomato Paste:**
   - Stir in chopped tomatoes and tomato paste. Cook for about 5 minutes until tomatoes break down and release their juices.
5. **Add Vegetables and Spices:**
   - Add diced carrots, diced green bell pepper, and chopped green beans to the pot.
   - Stir in ground ginger, ground coriander, ground cinnamon, ground cloves, ground nutmeg, salt, and pepper. Mix well to combine with the aromatics.
6. **Combine Rice and Meat:**

- - Return the browned meat to the pot, along with any juices.
  - Add rinsed rice to the pot and stir to coat the rice with the vegetable and spice mixture.
7. **Cook Riz Gras:**
   - Pour in beef or chicken broth, enough to cover the rice and meat mixture. Bring the mixture to a boil.
8. **Simmer the Dish:**
   - Reduce the heat to low. Cover the pot and let the Riz Gras simmer gently for about 20-25 minutes, or until the rice is tender and has absorbed the liquid. Stir occasionally to prevent sticking.
9. **Finish and Serve:**
   - Taste and adjust seasoning with salt and pepper if needed.
   - Garnish Burkina Faso's Riz Gras with chopped fresh parsley or cilantro before serving.
   - Serve hot as a main dish, accompanied by a side of salad or steamed vegetables.

Enjoy the aromatic flavors and hearty textures of Burkina Faso's Riz Gras, a dish that embodies the rich culinary heritage of West Africa!

Central African Republic's Kanda (Peanut Butter and Spinach Stew)

Ingredients:

- 500g chicken thighs, cut into pieces (you can also use beef, fish, or shrimp)
- 1 onion, finely chopped
- 3 cloves garlic, minced
- 2 tomatoes, chopped
- 1 cup peanut butter (smooth or crunchy)
- 4 cups fresh spinach leaves, chopped (you can also use cassava leaves if available)
- 2 tablespoons vegetable oil
- 1 tablespoon tomato paste
- 1 teaspoon ground ginger
- 1 teaspoon ground coriander
- 1/2 teaspoon ground cinnamon
- 1/4 teaspoon ground cloves
- 1/4 teaspoon cayenne pepper (optional, for heat)
- Salt and pepper to taste
- 4 cups chicken broth or water
- Fresh parsley or cilantro, chopped, for garnish
- Cooked rice or fufu (for serving)

Instructions:

1. **Prepare the Meat:**
    - Heat vegetable oil in a large pot or Dutch oven over medium-high heat.
    - Add the chicken pieces and brown them on all sides. Remove from the pot and set aside.
2. **Sauté Aromatics:**
    - In the same pot, add chopped onion and sauté until softened and translucent, about 5 minutes.
    - Add minced garlic and sauté for another 1-2 minutes until fragrant.
3. **Add Tomatoes and Tomato Paste:**
    - Stir in chopped tomatoes and tomato paste. Cook for about 5 minutes until tomatoes break down and release their juices.
4. **Prepare Peanut Butter Mixture:**
    - In a bowl, whisk together peanut butter with a cup of chicken broth or water until smooth. Set aside.
5. **Combine Ingredients:**
    - Return the browned chicken (or other meat/fish) to the pot with the aromatics.
    - Pour in the peanut butter mixture and remaining chicken broth or water. Stir well to combine.
6. **Add Spices and Greens:**

- Add ground ginger, ground coriander, ground cinnamon, ground cloves, cayenne pepper (if using), salt, and pepper. Stir to incorporate.

7. **Simmer Kanda:**
   - Bring the mixture to a boil, then reduce the heat to low. Cover the pot and let it simmer gently for about 30-40 minutes, stirring occasionally.
8. **Add Spinach:**
   - Stir in chopped spinach leaves (or cassava leaves if using). Cook for an additional 10-15 minutes, or until the spinach is wilted and tender.
9. **Finish and Serve:**
   - Taste and adjust seasoning with salt and pepper if needed.
   - Garnish Central African Republic's Kanda with chopped fresh parsley or cilantro before serving.
   - Serve hot with cooked rice or fufu, a traditional African starchy side dish.

Enjoy the creamy and nutty flavors of Central African Republic's Kanda, a comforting and nutritious stew that's perfect for sharing with family and friends!

Equatorial Guinean Chicken Muamba (Chicken and Palm Butter Stew)

Ingredients:

- 1 whole chicken, cut into pieces (or use chicken thighs and drumsticks)
- 1 onion, finely chopped
- 3 cloves garlic, minced
- 2 tomatoes, chopped
- 1 cup palm butter (red palm oil), preferably natural and unsalted
- 1 green bell pepper, chopped
- 1 red bell pepper, chopped
- 2 carrots, peeled and sliced
- 2 potatoes, peeled and cubed
- 2 cups chicken broth or water
- 1 tablespoon tomato paste
- 1 tablespoon ground dried shrimp (optional, for added flavor)
- 1 teaspoon ground ginger
- 1 teaspoon ground coriander
- 1/2 teaspoon ground cinnamon
- 1/4 teaspoon ground cloves
- Salt and pepper to taste
- Fresh parsley or cilantro, chopped, for garnish
- Cooked rice or fufu (for serving)

Instructions:

1. **Prepare the Chicken:**
    - Rinse the chicken pieces under cold water and pat dry with paper towels. Season with salt and pepper.
2. **Sauté the Chicken:**
    - Heat a large pot or Dutch oven over medium-high heat. Add a tablespoon of palm butter.
    - Add the chicken pieces and brown them on all sides. Remove from the pot and set aside.
3. **Sauté Aromatics:**
    - In the same pot, add chopped onion and sauté until softened and translucent, about 5-7 minutes.
    - Add minced garlic and sauté for another 1-2 minutes until fragrant.
4. **Add Tomatoes and Tomato Paste:**
    - Stir in chopped tomatoes and tomato paste. Cook for about 5 minutes until tomatoes break down and release their juices.
5. **Prepare Palm Butter Sauce:**
    - Add the remaining palm butter (red palm oil) to the pot. Stir well to combine with the aromatics.

6. **Add Vegetables and Spices:**
   - Add chopped green bell pepper, red bell pepper, sliced carrots, and cubed potatoes to the pot.
   - Stir in ground dried shrimp (if using), ground ginger, ground coriander, ground cinnamon, ground cloves, salt, and pepper. Mix well to combine.
7. **Simmer Chicken Muamba:**
   - Return the browned chicken pieces to the pot, along with any juices.
   - Pour in chicken broth or water, enough to cover the chicken and vegetables. Bring the mixture to a boil.
8. **Reduce Heat and Cook:**
   - Reduce the heat to low. Cover the pot and let Chicken Muamba simmer gently for about 45 minutes to 1 hour, or until the chicken is tender and cooked through, and the vegetables are soft.
9. **Finish and Serve:**
   - Taste and adjust seasoning with salt and pepper if needed.
   - Garnish Equatorial Guinean Chicken Muamba with chopped fresh parsley or cilantro before serving.
   - Serve hot with cooked rice or fufu, a traditional African starchy side dish.

Enjoy the rich and aromatic flavors of Equatorial Guinean Chicken Muamba, a dish that reflects the vibrant culinary heritage of Central Africa!

Guinea-Bissau's Canja de Galinha (Chicken and Rice Soup)

Ingredients:

- 1 whole chicken, cut into pieces (or use chicken thighs and drumsticks)
- 1 onion, finely chopped
- 3 cloves garlic, minced
- 2 tomatoes, chopped
- 1 cup white rice
- 1 carrot, peeled and diced
- 1 celery stalk, diced
- 1 bay leaf
- 1 teaspoon ground ginger
- 1/2 teaspoon ground turmeric
- Salt and pepper to taste
- Fresh parsley or cilantro, chopped, for garnish
- Lemon wedges, for serving

Instructions:

1. **Prepare the Chicken:**
    - Rinse the chicken pieces under cold water and pat dry with paper towels. Season with salt and pepper.
2. **Sauté the Chicken:**
    - In a large pot or Dutch oven, heat a tablespoon of vegetable oil over medium-high heat.
    - Add the chicken pieces and brown them on all sides. Remove from the pot and set aside.
3. **Sauté Aromatics:**
    - In the same pot, add chopped onion and sauté until softened and translucent, about 5-7 minutes.
    - Add minced garlic and sauté for another 1-2 minutes until fragrant.
4. **Add Tomatoes and Spices:**
    - Stir in chopped tomatoes and cook for about 5 minutes until tomatoes break down and release their juices.
    - Add ground ginger, ground turmeric, bay leaf, salt, and pepper. Mix well to combine with the aromatics.
5. **Cook the Soup:**
    - Return the browned chicken pieces to the pot, along with any juices.
    - Pour in enough water to cover the chicken pieces. Bring the mixture to a boil.
6. **Simmer the Soup:**
    - Reduce the heat to low. Cover the pot and let the soup simmer gently for about 30-40 minutes, or until the chicken is tender and cooked through.
7. **Add Rice and Vegetables:**

        - Add white rice, diced carrot, and diced celery to the pot. Stir well to combine.
        - Cook uncovered for another 15-20 minutes, or until the rice and vegetables are tender and the soup has thickened slightly.
8. **Finish and Serve:**
        - Taste and adjust seasoning with salt and pepper if needed.
        - Remove the bay leaf from the soup.
        - Garnish Canja de Galinha with chopped fresh parsley or cilantro before serving.
        - Serve hot with lemon wedges on the side for squeezing over the soup.

Enjoy the comforting and nourishing flavors of Guinea-Bissau's Canja de Galinha, a dish that warms the soul and brings a taste of West African cuisine to your table!

Lesotho's Moroho (Spinach and Potato Stew)

Ingredients:

- 500g spinach leaves, washed and chopped (you can also use Swiss chard or kale)
- 3 medium potatoes, peeled and diced
- 1 onion, finely chopped
- 2 tomatoes, chopped
- 3 tablespoons vegetable oil
- 2 cloves garlic, minced
- 1 teaspoon ground ginger
- 1 teaspoon ground paprika
- 1/2 teaspoon ground cumin
- Salt and pepper to taste
- Water or vegetable broth, as needed

Instructions:

1. **Prepare the Vegetables:**
   - Wash the spinach leaves thoroughly and chop them into smaller pieces. Set aside.
   - Peel and dice the potatoes into cubes. Set aside.
2. **Sauté the Onions and Garlic:**
   - Heat vegetable oil in a large pot or Dutch oven over medium heat.
   - Add chopped onion and sauté until softened and translucent, about 5-7 minutes.
   - Add minced garlic and sauté for another 1-2 minutes until fragrant.
3. **Add Tomatoes and Spices:**
   - Stir in chopped tomatoes and cook for about 5 minutes until tomatoes break down and release their juices.
   - Add ground ginger, ground paprika, ground cumin, salt, and pepper. Mix well to combine with the aromatics.
4. **Cook the Potatoes:**
   - Add diced potatoes to the pot. Stir well to coat the potatoes with the tomato and spice mixture.
   - Cook for about 5-7 minutes, stirring occasionally, until the potatoes begin to soften slightly.
5. **Add Spinach and Liquid:**
   - Add chopped spinach (or other greens) to the pot. Stir well to combine with the potatoes and spices.
   - If needed, add enough water or vegetable broth to just cover the vegetables.
6. **Simmer the Stew:**
   - Bring the mixture to a boil, then reduce the heat to low. Cover the pot and let the stew simmer gently for about 20-25 minutes, or until the potatoes are tender and cooked through.

7. **Adjust Seasoning and Serve:**
    - Taste and adjust seasoning with salt and pepper if needed.
    - Serve hot as a main dish, accompanied by bread or pap (a traditional South African maize porridge).

Moroho is a nutritious and satisfying dish that showcases the simple yet delicious flavors of Lesotho. It's perfect for a comforting meal that highlights fresh vegetables and warming spices.

Madagascar's Romazava (Meat and Leafy Greens Stew)

Ingredients:

- 500g beef stew meat, cut into cubes (you can also use lamb or pork)
- 1 onion, finely chopped
- 3 cloves garlic, minced
- 2 tomatoes, chopped
- 3 cups mixed leafy greens (spinach, kale, Swiss chard), chopped
- 2 cups green beans, trimmed and chopped
- 1 cup cabbage, chopped
- 2 carrots, peeled and sliced
- 2 potatoes, peeled and diced
- 2 tablespoons vegetable oil
- 1 tablespoon tomato paste
- 1 tablespoon soy sauce
- 1 teaspoon ground ginger
- 1 teaspoon ground coriander
- 1/2 teaspoon ground cloves
- 1/2 teaspoon ground black pepper
- Salt to taste
- Water or beef broth, as needed

Instructions:

1. **Prepare the Meat:**
   - Rinse the beef stew meat under cold water and pat dry with paper towels. Season with salt and pepper.
2. **Sauté the Meat:**
   - Heat vegetable oil in a large pot or Dutch oven over medium-high heat.
   - Add the beef cubes and brown them on all sides. Remove from the pot and set aside.
3. **Sauté Aromatics:**
   - In the same pot, add chopped onion and sauté until softened and translucent, about 5-7 minutes.
   - Add minced garlic and sauté for another 1-2 minutes until fragrant.
4. **Add Tomatoes and Tomato Paste:**
   - Stir in chopped tomatoes and tomato paste. Cook for about 5 minutes until tomatoes break down and release their juices.
5. **Cook the Vegetables:**
   - Add chopped mixed leafy greens, green beans, cabbage, carrots, and potatoes to the pot.
   - Stir in ground ginger, ground coriander, ground cloves, ground black pepper, soy sauce, and salt. Mix well to combine with the aromatics.

6. **Simmer the Stew:**
    - Return the browned beef cubes to the pot, along with any juices.
    - Add enough water or beef broth to cover the ingredients in the pot.
7. **Cook Until Tender:**
    - Bring the mixture to a boil, then reduce the heat to low. Cover the pot and let the Romazava simmer gently for about 1 to 1.5 hours, or until the meat and vegetables are tender and cooked through. Stir occasionally.
8. **Adjust Seasoning and Serve:**
    - Taste and adjust seasoning with salt and pepper if needed.
    - Serve hot as a main dish, accompanied by steamed rice or bread.

Romazava is a delightful and nutritious stew that captures the essence of Malagasy cuisine with its blend of meat, vegetables, and aromatic spices. Enjoy this flavorful dish with family and friends!

Mauritius' Daube (Beef Stew)

Ingredients:

- 1 kg beef chuck or stewing beef, cut into cubes
- 2 tablespoons vegetable oil
- 2 onions, finely chopped
- 3 cloves garlic, minced
- 2 tomatoes, chopped
- 2 tablespoons tomato paste
- 2 tablespoons Worcestershire sauce
- 2 tablespoons soy sauce
- 2 tablespoons red wine vinegar
- 2 cups beef broth or water
- 2 bay leaves
- 1 teaspoon dried thyme
- 1 teaspoon ground cloves
- 1 cinnamon stick
- Salt and pepper to taste
- Fresh parsley or cilantro, chopped, for garnish
- Cooked rice or mashed potatoes, for serving

Instructions:

1. **Brown the Beef:**
   - Heat vegetable oil in a large pot or Dutch oven over medium-high heat.
   - Add the beef cubes in batches and brown them on all sides. Remove from the pot and set aside.
2. **Sauté Aromatics:**
   - In the same pot, add chopped onions and sauté until softened and translucent, about 5-7 minutes.
   - Add minced garlic and sauté for another 1-2 minutes until fragrant.
3. **Add Tomatoes and Tomato Paste:**
   - Stir in chopped tomatoes and tomato paste. Cook for about 5 minutes until tomatoes break down and release their juices.
4. **Deglaze the Pot:**
   - Pour in Worcestershire sauce, soy sauce, and red wine vinegar. Scrape the bottom of the pot to loosen any browned bits (this adds flavor).
5. **Combine Beef and Broth:**
   - Return the browned beef cubes to the pot, along with any juices.
   - Add beef broth or water to the pot. Stir well to combine.
6. **Add Spices:**
   - Add bay leaves, dried thyme, ground cloves, and cinnamon stick to the pot. Season with salt and pepper to taste. Mix well.

7. **Simmer the Daube:**
   - Bring the mixture to a boil, then reduce the heat to low. Cover the pot and let the Daube simmer gently for about 2 to 2.5 hours, stirring occasionally, or until the beef is tender and the flavors have melded together.
8. **Finish and Serve:**
   - Taste and adjust seasoning with salt and pepper if needed.
   - Remove the cinnamon stick and bay leaves from the Daube.
   - Garnish Mauritian Daube with chopped fresh parsley or cilantro before serving.
   - Serve hot over cooked rice or mashed potatoes.

Enjoy the rich and savory flavors of Mauritian Daube, a delightful dish that brings warmth and comfort to any meal!

Mozambique's Matapa (Cassava Leaves and Peanut Stew)

Ingredients:

- 500g cassava leaves (fresh or frozen), chopped (substitute with spinach or kale if cassava leaves are unavailable)
- 1 cup unsweetened shredded coconut
- 1 cup ground peanuts or peanut butter
- 400ml coconut milk
- 500g shrimp, peeled and deveined (optional, can also use chicken or fish)
- 1 onion, finely chopped
- 3 cloves garlic, minced
- 2 tomatoes, chopped
- 2 tablespoons vegetable oil
- 1 tablespoon tomato paste
- 1 teaspoon ground ginger
- 1 teaspoon ground coriander
- 1/2 teaspoon ground turmeric
- 1/4 teaspoon ground cloves
- Salt and pepper to taste
- Fresh cilantro or parsley, chopped, for garnish
- Cooked rice, for serving

Instructions:

1. **Prepare the Cassava Leaves:**
   - If using fresh cassava leaves, wash them thoroughly and chop finely. If using frozen, thaw them according to package instructions.
2. **Prepare the Coconut Mixture:**
   - In a blender or food processor, blend shredded coconut with ground peanuts (or peanut butter) and coconut milk until smooth. Set aside.
3. **Sauté the Aromatics:**
   - Heat vegetable oil in a large pot or Dutch oven over medium heat.
   - Add chopped onion and sauté until softened and translucent, about 5-7 minutes.
   - Add minced garlic and sauté for another 1-2 minutes until fragrant.
4. **Add Tomatoes and Spices:**
   - Stir in chopped tomatoes and tomato paste. Cook for about 5 minutes until tomatoes break down and release their juices.
   - Add ground ginger, ground coriander, ground turmeric, ground cloves, salt, and pepper. Mix well to combine with the aromatics.
5. **Cook the Shrimp (or Protein):**
   - If using shrimp, add them to the pot and cook until pink and cooked through, about 3-5 minutes. If using chicken or fish, cook until no longer pink (or opaque for fish).

6. **Combine Cassava Leaves and Coconut Mixture:**
    - Add chopped cassava leaves to the pot, stirring well to coat with the onion and spice mixture.
    - Pour in the blended coconut mixture (from step 2) into the pot. Stir well to combine all ingredients.
7. **Simmer the Matapa:**
    - Bring the mixture to a boil, then reduce the heat to low. Cover the pot and let the Matapa simmer gently for about 30-40 minutes, stirring occasionally, or until the cassava leaves are tender and cooked through.
8. **Finish and Serve:**
    - Taste and adjust seasoning with salt and pepper if needed.
    - Garnish Mozambique's Matapa with chopped fresh cilantro or parsley before serving.
    - Serve hot over cooked rice, typically as a main dish.

Enjoy the creamy and nutty flavors of Matapa, a delicious representation of Mozambican cuisine that's perfect for sharing with family and friends!

Niger's Djerma Stew (Beef and Peanut Butter)

Ingredients:

- 500g beef stew meat, cut into cubes
- 1 onion, finely chopped
- 3 cloves garlic, minced
- 2 tomatoes, chopped
- 1 cup peanut butter (smooth or chunky)
- 2 cups beef broth or water
- 2 tablespoons vegetable oil
- 1 tablespoon tomato paste
- 1 teaspoon ground ginger
- 1 teaspoon ground coriander
- 1/2 teaspoon ground cumin
- 1/4 teaspoon cayenne pepper (optional, for heat)
- Salt and pepper to taste
- 2-3 potatoes, peeled and diced
- 2 carrots, peeled and sliced
- Fresh cilantro or parsley, chopped, for garnish
- Cooked rice or millet, for serving

Instructions:

1. **Brown the Beef:**
   - Heat vegetable oil in a large pot or Dutch oven over medium-high heat.
   - Add the beef cubes in batches and brown them on all sides. Remove from the pot and set aside.
2. **Sauté Aromatics:**
   - In the same pot, add chopped onion and sauté until softened and translucent, about 5-7 minutes.
   - Add minced garlic and sauté for another 1-2 minutes until fragrant.
3. **Add Tomatoes and Tomato Paste:**
   - Stir in chopped tomatoes and tomato paste. Cook for about 5 minutes until tomatoes break down and release their juices.
4. **Prepare Peanut Butter Mixture:**
   - In a bowl, whisk together peanut butter with beef broth or water until smooth. Set aside.
5. **Combine Ingredients:**
   - Return the browned beef cubes to the pot, along with any juices.
   - Pour in the peanut butter mixture into the pot. Stir well to combine.
6. **Add Spices and Vegetables:**
   - Add ground ginger, ground coriander, ground cumin, cayenne pepper (if using), salt, and pepper. Mix well.

- Add diced potatoes and sliced carrots to the pot. Stir to combine with the stew.
7. **Simmer the Stew:**
    - Bring the stew to a boil, then reduce the heat to low. Cover the pot and let it simmer gently for about 1 to 1.5 hours, stirring occasionally, or until the beef is tender and cooked through, and the vegetables are soft.
8. **Adjust Seasoning and Serve:**
    - Taste and adjust seasoning with salt and pepper if needed.
    - Garnish Niger's Djerma Stew with chopped fresh cilantro or parsley before serving.
    - Serve hot over cooked rice or millet, a traditional grain in Nigerien cuisine.

Enjoy the rich and nutty flavors of Djerma Stew, a comforting and hearty dish that's perfect for a satisfying meal!

Sao Tome and Principe's Calulu de Peixe (Fish Stew)

Ingredients:

- 500g firm white fish fillets (such as cod, haddock, or tilapia), cut into chunks
- 1 onion, finely chopped
- 3 cloves garlic, minced
- 2 tomatoes, chopped
- 1 green bell pepper, chopped
- 1 red bell pepper, chopped
- 1 carrot, peeled and sliced
- 1 potato, peeled and diced
- 1 eggplant, diced
- 1 cup okra, sliced (fresh or frozen)
- 2 cups fish or vegetable broth
- 1 cup coconut milk
- 2 tablespoons tomato paste
- 2 tablespoons palm oil (dende oil), optional for authentic flavor
- 2 tablespoons vegetable oil
- 1 tablespoon ground dried shrimp or fish powder (optional, for added flavor)
- 1 teaspoon ground ginger
- 1 teaspoon paprika
- 1/2 teaspoon ground black pepper
- Salt to taste
- Fresh parsley or cilantro, chopped, for garnish
- Cooked rice or bread, for serving

Instructions:

1. **Prepare the Fish:**
   - Rinse the fish fillets under cold water and pat dry with paper towels. Cut into bite-sized chunks. Season lightly with salt and pepper.
2. **Sauté Aromatics:**
   - Heat vegetable oil in a large pot or Dutch oven over medium heat.
   - Add chopped onion and sauté until softened and translucent, about 5-7 minutes.
   - Add minced garlic and sauté for another 1-2 minutes until fragrant.
3. **Add Tomatoes and Spices:**
   - Stir in chopped tomatoes, green bell pepper, and red bell pepper. Cook for about 5 minutes until vegetables begin to soften.
   - Add tomato paste, ground ginger, paprika, ground black pepper, and salt. Mix well to combine.
4. **Add Vegetables and Broth:**
   - Add sliced carrot, diced potato, diced eggplant, and sliced okra to the pot.

- Pour in fish or vegetable broth and coconut milk. Stir well to combine all ingredients.
5. **Simmer the Stew:**
    - Bring the mixture to a boil, then reduce the heat to low. Cover the pot and let the stew simmer gently for about 15-20 minutes, or until the vegetables are tender.
6. **Add Fish and Palm Oil:**
    - Add the fish chunks to the pot, gently stirring to submerge them in the stew.
    - If using palm oil (dende oil), add it at this stage for an authentic flavor. Stir well.
7. **Cook Fish and Adjust Seasoning:**
    - Let the stew simmer for another 5-10 minutes, or until the fish is cooked through and flakes easily with a fork.
    - Taste and adjust seasoning with salt and pepper if needed.
8. **Finish and Serve:**
    - Remove from heat. Garnish Calulu de Peixe with chopped fresh parsley or cilantro before serving.
    - Serve hot over cooked rice or with bread, allowing the flavors to meld together.

Enjoy the delightful flavors of São Tomé and Príncipe's Calulu de Peixe, a dish that captures the essence of island cuisine with its blend of fish, vegetables, and spices!

Seychelles' Kat-kat Banane (Plantain Stew)

Ingredients:

- 3 ripe plantains
- 1 onion, finely chopped
- 2 tomatoes, chopped
- 3 cloves garlic, minced
- 1 cup coconut milk
- 1 cup vegetable broth or water
- 200g shrimp or chicken breast, diced (optional)
- 2 tablespoons vegetable oil
- 1 tablespoon tomato paste
- 1 teaspoon ground ginger
- 1 teaspoon ground coriander
- 1/2 teaspoon ground turmeric
- 1/4 teaspoon ground cloves
- Salt and pepper to taste
- Fresh cilantro or parsley, chopped, for garnish
- Cooked rice or bread, for serving

Instructions:

1. **Prepare the Plantains:**
   - Peel the ripe plantains and cut them into slices. You can cut them into rounds or diagonal slices, as preferred. Set aside.
2. **Sauté Aromatics:**
   - Heat vegetable oil in a large pot or Dutch oven over medium heat.
   - Add chopped onion and sauté until softened and translucent, about 5-7 minutes.
   - Add minced garlic and sauté for another 1-2 minutes until fragrant.
3. **Add Tomatoes and Spices:**
   - Stir in chopped tomatoes and tomato paste. Cook for about 5 minutes until tomatoes soften and release their juices.
   - Add ground ginger, ground coriander, ground turmeric, ground cloves, salt, and pepper. Mix well to combine with the aromatics.
4. **Add Coconut Milk and Broth:**
   - Pour in coconut milk and vegetable broth or water. Stir well to combine all ingredients. Bring the mixture to a gentle simmer.
5. **Cook the Plantains (and Meat/Seafood, if using):**
   - Add the sliced plantains to the pot, stirring gently to coat them with the sauce. If you are using shrimp or diced chicken breast, add them to the pot at this stage. Stir well to combine.
6. **Simmer Until Tender:**

- Reduce the heat to low and let the stew simmer gently for about 15-20 minutes, or until the plantains are tender and cooked through. Stir occasionally to prevent sticking.
7. **Adjust Seasoning:**
    - Taste and adjust the seasoning with salt and pepper if needed. If you prefer a spicier stew, you can add more ground black pepper or a pinch of cayenne pepper.
8. **Serve:**
    - Once the plantains are tender and the flavors have melded together, remove the pot from heat.
    - Garnish Seychelles' Kat-kat Banane with chopped fresh cilantro or parsley before serving.
    - Serve hot over cooked rice or with crusty bread to soak up the delicious sauce.

Enjoy the comforting and tropical flavors of Kat-kat Banane from Seychelles, a dish that brings together the sweetness of ripe plantains with the richness of coconut milk and spices!

South Sudan's Kisra (Sorghum Flatbread) with Stew

Ingredients:

- 2 cups sorghum flour
- 1 cup all-purpose flour
- 1 teaspoon salt
- 3 cups water (approximately), divided
- Vegetable oil, for cooking

Instructions:

1. **Mix the Flours and Salt:**
    - In a large bowl, combine the sorghum flour, all-purpose flour, and salt.
2. **Make the Batter:**
    - Gradually add 2 cups of water to the flour mixture, stirring constantly to form a smooth batter. The consistency should be similar to pancake batter. Add more water if needed.
3. **Ferment the Batter:**
    - Cover the bowl with a clean cloth and let it sit at room temperature for 1-2 days to ferment. The batter should develop a slightly sour taste and bubbles on the surface.
4. **Cook the Kisra:**
    - Heat a non-stick skillet or griddle over medium heat. Lightly grease the surface with vegetable oil.
    - Pour a ladleful of the batter onto the skillet and spread it into a thin, even layer using the back of the ladle or a spatula.
    - Cook for 2-3 minutes on one side until bubbles form on the surface and the edges start to lift. Flip and cook for another 1-2 minutes on the other side until golden brown spots appear.
    - Repeat with the remaining batter, stacking the cooked flatbreads and covering them with a clean cloth to keep warm.

South Sudanese Stew (Meat or Vegetable)

Ingredients:

- 500g beef, lamb, or chicken, cut into cubes (or substitute with lentils or chickpeas for a vegetarian version)
- 1 onion, finely chopped
- 3 cloves garlic, minced
- 2 tomatoes, chopped
- 2 tablespoons tomato paste
- 2 cups vegetable or meat broth
- 1 cup chopped spinach or kale (optional)

- 1 tablespoon vegetable oil
- 1 teaspoon ground cumin
- 1 teaspoon ground coriander
- 1/2 teaspoon ground turmeric
- Salt and pepper to taste

Instructions:

1. **Sauté Aromatics:**
   - Heat vegetable oil in a large pot or Dutch oven over medium heat.
   - Add chopped onion and sauté until softened and translucent, about 5-7 minutes.
   - Add minced garlic and sauté for another 1-2 minutes until fragrant.
2. **Brown the Meat (if using):**
   - Add the cubed meat to the pot and cook until browned on all sides.
3. **Add Tomatoes and Spices:**
   - Stir in chopped tomatoes and tomato paste. Cook for about 5 minutes until tomatoes break down and release their juices.
   - Add ground cumin, ground coriander, ground turmeric, salt, and pepper. Mix well to combine.
4. **Simmer the Stew:**
   - Pour in vegetable or meat broth to the pot. Bring to a boil, then reduce the heat to low. Cover and let the stew simmer gently for about 1 hour, stirring occasionally, or until the meat is tender (or vegetables are cooked through for vegetarian version).
5. **Add Greens (if using):**
   - If using chopped spinach or kale, add them to the stew during the last 10 minutes of cooking. Stir well to combine and cook until wilted.
6. **Serve:**
   - Serve the South Sudanese stew hot with the Kisra flatbread.

Enjoy the hearty and comforting flavors of South Sudan's Kisra with Stew, a traditional dish that brings together the nutty sorghum flatbread with a rich and flavorful stew!

Swaziland's Siswati Stew (Meat and Vegetables)

Ingredients:

- 500g beef or goat meat, cubed
- 2 onions, finely chopped
- 3 cloves garlic, minced
- 2 tomatoes, chopped
- 2 carrots, peeled and sliced
- 2 potatoes, peeled and diced
- 1 cup green beans, trimmed and cut into pieces
- 1 cup cabbage, shredded
- 2 tablespoons vegetable oil
- 2 cups beef or vegetable broth
- 2 tablespoons tomato paste
- 1 teaspoon ground cumin
- 1 teaspoon ground coriander
- 1/2 teaspoon ground turmeric
- Salt and pepper to taste
- Fresh cilantro or parsley, chopped, for garnish
- Cooked rice or pap (maize porridge), for serving

Instructions:

1. **Brown the Meat:**
    - Heat vegetable oil in a large pot or Dutch oven over medium-high heat.
    - Add the cubed meat and brown on all sides. Remove from the pot and set aside.
2. **Sauté Aromatics:**
    - In the same pot, add chopped onions and sauté until softened and translucent, about 5-7 minutes.
    - Add minced garlic and sauté for another 1-2 minutes until fragrant.
3. **Add Tomatoes and Spices:**
    - Stir in chopped tomatoes and tomato paste. Cook for about 5 minutes until tomatoes break down and release their juices.
    - Add ground cumin, ground coriander, ground turmeric, salt, and pepper. Mix well to combine with the aromatics.
4. **Simmer the Stew:**
    - Return the browned meat to the pot.
    - Pour in beef or vegetable broth. Stir well to combine all ingredients.
5. **Add Vegetables:**
    - Add sliced carrots, diced potatoes, green beans, and shredded cabbage to the pot. Stir to combine with the stew.
6. **Cook Until Tender:**

- Bring the stew to a boil, then reduce the heat to low. Cover the pot and let it simmer gently for about 1 to 1.5 hours, or until the meat is tender and the vegetables are cooked through. Stir occasionally to prevent sticking.
7. **Adjust Seasoning and Serve:**
    - Taste and adjust seasoning with salt and pepper if needed.
    - Garnish Swaziland's Siswati Stew with chopped fresh cilantro or parsley before serving.
    - Serve hot over cooked rice or pap (maize porridge), a traditional accompaniment in Swazi cuisine.

Enjoy the rich flavors and hearty goodness of Siswati Stew (Liphofu), a delicious representation of Swaziland's culinary heritage!

Togo's Fufu and Sauce Claire (Peanut Sauce)

Ingredients:

- 2 cups cassava flour (or yam flour or plantain flour)
- Water
- Salt (optional)

Instructions:

1. **Prepare the Fufu Dough:**
   - In a large bowl, add the cassava flour (or your preferred flour).
   - Gradually add water while mixing with your hands or a wooden spoon until a smooth, soft dough is formed. The consistency should be similar to firm mashed potatoes.
2. **Cook the Fufu:**
   - Transfer the dough to a large pot or saucepan. Add enough water to cover the dough.
   - Bring to a boil over medium-high heat, stirring constantly to prevent lumps. Reduce the heat to low and simmer for 10-15 minutes, stirring occasionally, until the fufu is smooth and thickened.
3. **Shape the Fufu:**
   - Wet your hands with water to prevent sticking, then scoop out a portion of the fufu dough and shape it into a smooth ball or mound.

Sauce Claire (Peanut Sauce)

Ingredients:

- 1 cup smooth peanut butter
- 2 cups vegetable or chicken broth
- 1 onion, finely chopped
- 2 tomatoes, chopped
- 3 cloves garlic, minced
- 1 tablespoon tomato paste
- 1 teaspoon ground ginger
- 1 teaspoon ground coriander
- 1/2 teaspoon cayenne pepper (optional, for heat)
- Salt and pepper to taste
- Vegetable oil for cooking

Instructions:

1. **Sauté Aromatics:**
   - Heat vegetable oil in a large skillet or saucepan over medium heat.

- Add chopped onion and sauté until softened and translucent, about 5-7 minutes.
- Add minced garlic and sauté for another 1-2 minutes until fragrant.

2. **Prepare the Peanut Sauce:**
    - Stir in chopped tomatoes and tomato paste. Cook for about 5 minutes until tomatoes break down and release their juices.
    - Add ground ginger, ground coriander, cayenne pepper (if using), salt, and pepper. Mix well to combine with the aromatics.
3. **Add Peanut Butter and Broth:**
    - Add smooth peanut butter to the skillet, stirring continuously to combine with the onion and tomato mixture.
    - Gradually add vegetable or chicken broth, stirring constantly to create a smooth sauce. Adjust the amount of broth to achieve the desired consistency.
4. **Simmer the Sauce:**
    - Bring the sauce to a gentle simmer. Reduce heat to low and let it simmer for about 10-15 minutes, stirring occasionally, until the flavors meld together and the sauce thickens slightly.
5. **Serve:**
    - Serve the Fufu and Sauce Claire hot. Place a portion of fufu on each plate or bowl, and ladle the peanut sauce over the fufu.
6. **Optional Garnishes:**
    - Garnish with chopped fresh cilantro or parsley before serving for added flavor and freshness.

Enjoy the delicious and comforting flavors of Togo's Fufu and Sauce Claire, a dish that combines creamy peanut sauce with a soft, doughy fufu, creating a delightful harmony of textures and tastes!

Zambia's Chikanda (Wild Orchid Tubers Stew)

Ingredients:

- 500g wild orchid tubers (Disa species) or substitute with chickpea flour or groundnuts (peanuts)
- 1 onion, finely chopped
- 3 cloves garlic, minced
- 2 tomatoes, chopped
- 1 cup spinach, chopped
- 2 cups vegetable broth or water
- 2 tablespoons vegetable oil
- 1 tablespoon tomato paste
- 1 teaspoon ground coriander
- 1/2 teaspoon ground cumin
- 1/2 teaspoon ground turmeric
- Salt and pepper to taste
- Fresh cilantro or parsley, chopped, for garnish
- Cooked rice or bread, for serving

Instructions:

1. **Prepare the Ingredients:**
   - If using wild orchid tubers, peel and grate them finely. Alternatively, if not available, you can use chickpea flour or groundnuts (peanuts) as a substitute.
2. **Sauté Aromatics:**
   - Heat vegetable oil in a large pot or Dutch oven over medium heat.
   - Add chopped onion and sauté until softened and translucent, about 5-7 minutes.
   - Add minced garlic and sauté for another 1-2 minutes until fragrant.
3. **Add Tomatoes and Spices:**
   - Stir in chopped tomatoes and tomato paste. Cook for about 5 minutes until tomatoes break down and release their juices.
   - Add ground coriander, ground cumin, ground turmeric, salt, and pepper. Mix well to combine with the aromatics.
4. **Prepare Chikanda Mixture:**
   - If using wild orchid tubers, add them to the pot and stir to combine with the tomato mixture. If using chickpea flour or groundnuts, gradually add them while stirring to avoid lumps.
5. **Add Spinach and Broth:**
   - Add chopped spinach to the pot. Pour in vegetable broth or water, stirring continuously to create a smooth consistency. Adjust the amount of liquid as needed.
6. **Simmer the Stew:**

- Bring the mixture to a boil, then reduce the heat to low. Cover the pot and let the stew simmer gently for about 20-30 minutes, stirring occasionally, until the flavors meld together and the stew thickens.

7. **Adjust Seasoning and Serve:**
    - Taste and adjust seasoning with salt and pepper if needed.
    - Garnish Zambia's Chikanda with chopped fresh cilantro or parsley before serving.
    - Serve hot over cooked rice or with bread, enjoying the unique flavors of this traditional Zambian dish.

Note: Chikanda is traditionally shaped into logs or sausages and then steamed or boiled before slicing and serving. However, due to the sensitive nature of wild orchid tubers, consider exploring alternatives such as chickpea flour or groundnuts for a more sustainable approach to making this dish.

Botswana's Seswaa (Shredded Beef Stew)

Ingredients:

- 1 kg beef (preferably a tough cut like chuck roast), cut into large chunks
- 2 onions, finely chopped
- 3 cloves garlic, minced
- 2 tomatoes, chopped
- 2 cups beef broth or water
- 2 tablespoons vegetable oil
- Salt and pepper to taste
- Fresh cilantro or parsley, chopped, for garnish
- Cooked maize porridge (pap) or rice, for serving

Instructions:

1. **Brown the Beef:**
   - Heat vegetable oil in a large pot or Dutch oven over medium-high heat.
   - Add the beef chunks in batches and brown them on all sides. This adds flavor to the stew. Remove each batch and set aside.
2. **Sauté Aromatics:**
   - In the same pot, add chopped onions and sauté until softened and translucent, about 5-7 minutes.
   - Add minced garlic and sauté for another 1-2 minutes until fragrant.
3. **Add Tomatoes and Beef:**
   - Stir in chopped tomatoes and cook for about 5 minutes until they soften.
   - Return the browned beef chunks to the pot. Stir to combine with the onions and tomatoes.
4. **Simmer the Stew:**
   - Pour in beef broth or water, enough to cover the beef chunks. Bring to a boil.
5. **Cook Until Tender:**
   - Reduce the heat to low, cover the pot, and let the stew simmer gently for about 2-3 hours, or until the beef is very tender and can be easily shredded with a fork.
6. **Shred the Beef:**
   - Once the beef is tender, remove the pot from heat. Using two forks or a potato masher, shred the beef into fine strands. This process gives Seswaa its characteristic texture.
7. **Adjust Seasoning and Serve:**
   - Taste the stew and adjust seasoning with salt and pepper as needed.
   - Garnish Botswana's Seswaa with chopped fresh cilantro or parsley before serving.
   - Serve hot over cooked maize porridge (pap) or rice, allowing the flavors to meld together.

Enjoy the rich and comforting flavors of Botswana's Seswaa (Shredded Beef Stew), a dish that showcases the delicious simplicity of slow-cooked beef with aromatic spices and herbs!

Comoros' Langouste a la Vanille (Lobster in Vanilla Sauce)

Ingredients:

- 2 lobsters, about 500g each (or use lobster tails)
- 2 tablespoons butter
- 1 onion, finely chopped
- 2 cloves garlic, minced
- 2 tomatoes, chopped
- 1 cup coconut milk
- 1 vanilla bean, split lengthwise
- Juice of 1 lemon
- Salt and pepper to taste
- Fresh parsley or cilantro, chopped, for garnish
- Cooked rice or crusty bread, for serving

Instructions:

1. **Prepare the Lobster:**
   - If using whole lobsters, parboil them for 5 minutes in salted water. Remove from water and let them cool slightly. Cut the lobsters in half lengthwise and remove the meat from the shells. Cut the lobster meat into large chunks. If using lobster tails, remove the meat from the shells and cut into chunks.
2. **Sauté Aromatics:**
   - In a large skillet or saucepan, melt the butter over medium heat.
   - Add chopped onion and sauté until softened and translucent, about 5 minutes.
   - Add minced garlic and sauté for another 1-2 minutes until fragrant.
3. **Add Tomatoes and Vanilla:**
   - Stir in chopped tomatoes and cook for about 5 minutes until they start to soften.
   - Scrape the seeds from the vanilla bean and add both the seeds and the pod to the skillet. This will infuse the sauce with the vanilla flavor. Stir to combine.
4. **Cook the Lobster:**
   - Add the lobster meat to the skillet. Cook for about 2-3 minutes, stirring gently, until the lobster meat starts to turn opaque.
5. **Add Coconut Milk:**
   - Pour in the coconut milk and stir well to combine with the lobster and aromatics. Bring to a gentle simmer.
6. **Simmer and Season:**
   - Reduce the heat to low and let the sauce simmer gently for about 5-7 minutes, or until the lobster is fully cooked and tender. Be careful not to overcook the lobster.
7. **Finish and Serve:**
   - Squeeze lemon juice over the lobster and sauce. Season with salt and pepper to taste.
   - Garnish Comoros' Langouste à la Vanille with chopped fresh parsley or cilantro.

- - Serve hot over cooked rice or with crusty bread to soak up the delicious vanilla-infused coconut sauce.

Enjoy the luxurious flavors of Langouste à la Vanille, a dish that brings together the sweetness of lobster with the aromatic richness of vanilla and coconut milk, reflecting the culinary delights of Comoros!

Djibouti's Fah-fah (Lamb and Yogurt Stew)

Ingredients:

- 1 kg lamb, cut into cubes (you can also use beef or goat)
- 2 onions, finely chopped
- 3 cloves garlic, minced
- 2 tomatoes, chopped
- 1 cup plain yogurt
- 2 cups water or beef broth
- 2 tablespoons vegetable oil
- 1 tablespoon tomato paste
- 1 teaspoon ground cumin
- 1 teaspoon ground coriander
- 1/2 teaspoon ground turmeric
- 1/4 teaspoon ground cinnamon
- Salt and pepper to taste
- Fresh cilantro or parsley, chopped, for garnish
- Cooked rice or bread, for serving

Instructions:

1. **Brown the Lamb:**
   - Heat vegetable oil in a large pot or Dutch oven over medium-high heat.
   - Add the lamb cubes in batches and brown them on all sides. Remove each batch and set aside.
2. **Sauté Aromatics:**
   - In the same pot, add chopped onions and sauté until softened and translucent, about 5-7 minutes.
   - Add minced garlic and sauté for another 1-2 minutes until fragrant.
3. **Add Tomatoes and Spices:**
   - Stir in chopped tomatoes and tomato paste. Cook for about 5 minutes until tomatoes break down and release their juices.
   - Add ground cumin, ground coriander, ground turmeric, ground cinnamon, salt, and pepper. Mix well to combine with the aromatics.
4. **Simmer the Stew:**
   - Return the browned lamb cubes to the pot.
   - Pour in water or beef broth, enough to cover the lamb cubes. Stir well to combine.
5. **Cook Until Tender:**
   - Bring the stew to a boil, then reduce the heat to low. Cover the pot and let it simmer gently for about 1.5 to 2 hours, or until the lamb is tender and cooked through. Stir occasionally.
6. **Add Yogurt:**

    - Gradually add plain yogurt to the stew, stirring continuously to incorporate it into the sauce. This adds creaminess and tanginess to the dish.
7. **Simmer and Adjust Seasoning:**
    - Let the stew simmer for another 10-15 minutes to allow the flavors to meld together and the sauce to thicken slightly.
    - Taste and adjust seasoning with salt and pepper if needed.
8. **Serve:**
    - Garnish Djibouti's Fah-fah with chopped fresh cilantro or parsley before serving.
    - Serve hot over cooked rice or with bread, enjoying the rich and comforting flavors of this traditional Djiboutian stew.

Enjoy the delicious and aromatic Fah-fah (Lamb and Yogurt Stew), a dish that reflects the vibrant culinary heritage of Djibouti!

Guinea's Mafé (Peanut Sauce with Meat)

Ingredients:

- 500g beef or lamb, cut into cubes (you can also use chicken or goat)
- 2 tablespoons vegetable oil
- 1 onion, finely chopped
- 3 cloves garlic, minced
- 2 tomatoes, chopped
- 1 cup peanut butter (smooth or chunky)
- 2 cups beef or vegetable broth
- 2 cups chopped vegetables (such as carrots, potatoes, and bell peppers)
- 1 tablespoon tomato paste
- 1 teaspoon ground cumin
- 1 teaspoon ground coriander
- 1/2 teaspoon cayenne pepper (optional, for heat)
- Salt and pepper to taste
- Fresh cilantro or parsley, chopped, for garnish
- Cooked rice or couscous, for serving

Instructions:

1. **Brown the Meat:**
   - Heat vegetable oil in a large pot or Dutch oven over medium-high heat.
   - Add the beef or lamb cubes and brown them on all sides. Remove from the pot and set aside.
2. **Sauté Aromatics:**
   - In the same pot, add chopped onion and sauté until softened and translucent, about 5-7 minutes.
   - Add minced garlic and sauté for another 1-2 minutes until fragrant.
3. **Add Tomatoes and Spices:**
   - Stir in chopped tomatoes and tomato paste. Cook for about 5 minutes until tomatoes break down and release their juices.
   - Add ground cumin, ground coriander, cayenne pepper (if using), salt, and pepper. Mix well to combine with the aromatics.
4. **Prepare the Peanut Sauce:**
   - Add peanut butter to the pot, stirring continuously to combine with the onion and tomato mixture.
   - Gradually add beef or vegetable broth, stirring constantly to create a smooth sauce. Adjust the amount of broth to achieve the desired consistency.
5. **Simmer the Sauce:**
   - Return the browned meat to the pot. Bring the sauce to a gentle simmer over medium-low heat.

- Cover the pot and let it simmer for about 1.5 to 2 hours, or until the meat is tender and cooked through. Stir occasionally.
6. **Add Vegetables:**
   - Add chopped vegetables (such as carrots, potatoes, and bell peppers) to the pot. Stir well to combine with the sauce.
7. **Continue Simmering:**
   - Let the Mafé simmer for another 15-20 minutes, or until the vegetables are tender and the sauce has thickened. Adjust seasoning with salt and pepper if needed.
8. **Serve:**
   - Garnish Guinea's Mafé with chopped fresh cilantro or parsley before serving.
   - Serve hot over cooked rice or couscous, allowing the flavors to meld together.

Enjoy the delicious and comforting flavors of Guinea's Mafé, a dish that showcases the richness of peanut butter combined with tender meat and vibrant vegetables!

Kenya's Githeri (Maize and Beans Stew)

Ingredients:

- 1 cup dried maize (corn), soaked overnight (or use canned corn kernels)
- 1 cup dried beans (such as kidney beans or black-eyed peas), soaked overnight (or use canned beans)
- 2 tablespoons vegetable oil
- 1 onion, finely chopped
- 3 cloves garlic, minced
- 2 tomatoes, chopped
- 1 cup chopped vegetables (such as carrots, green beans, peas)
- 1 tablespoon tomato paste
- 1 teaspoon ground cumin
- 1 teaspoon ground coriander
- 1/2 teaspoon turmeric powder
- 1/2 teaspoon paprika (optional, for added spice)
- Salt and pepper to taste
- Fresh cilantro or parsley, chopped, for garnish

Instructions:

1. **Prepare the Maize and Beans:**
   - If using dried maize and beans, soak them separately in water overnight. Drain and rinse before cooking. Alternatively, you can use canned corn kernels and canned beans, which don't require soaking.
2. **Cook the Maize and Beans:**
   - In a large pot, bring water to a boil. Add the soaked maize and beans (or canned corn and beans) to the pot.
   - Reduce the heat to medium-low and simmer for about 1 to 1.5 hours, or until the maize and beans are tender. Drain and set aside.
3. **Sauté Aromatics:**
   - Heat vegetable oil in a large skillet or saucepan over medium heat.
   - Add chopped onion and sauté until softened and translucent, about 5-7 minutes.
   - Add minced garlic and sauté for another 1-2 minutes until fragrant.
4. **Add Tomatoes and Spices:**
   - Stir in chopped tomatoes and tomato paste. Cook for about 5 minutes until tomatoes break down and release their juices.
   - Add ground cumin, ground coriander, turmeric powder, paprika (if using), salt, and pepper. Mix well to combine with the aromatics.
5. **Combine Maize, Beans, and Vegetables:**
   - Add the cooked maize and beans (or canned corn and beans) to the skillet with the tomato mixture.

- Stir in chopped vegetables (such as carrots, green beans, and peas). Mix well to combine all ingredients.

6. **Simmer Githeri:**
    - Pour in a little water or vegetable broth if needed to create a stew-like consistency.
    - Cover the skillet or saucepan, reduce the heat to low, and let the Githeri simmer gently for about 15-20 minutes, or until the vegetables are tender and the flavors have melded together.

7. **Adjust Seasoning and Serve:**
    - Taste and adjust seasoning with salt and pepper if needed.
    - Garnish Kenya's Githeri with chopped fresh cilantro or parsley before serving.
    - Serve hot as a main dish, optionally with a side of chapati (flatbread) or ugali (maize porridge), for a complete and satisfying meal.

Enjoy the wholesome and comforting flavors of Githeri, a dish that embodies the traditional cuisine of Kenya with its simple yet hearty combination of maize, beans, and vegetables!

Liberia's Palava Sauce

Ingredients:

- 500g meat (chicken, beef, or goat), cut into cubes
- 1 large onion, chopped
- 3 cloves garlic, minced
- 2 tomatoes, chopped
- 2 cups chopped leafy greens (spinach, collard greens, or a combination)
- 1 cup peanut butter (smooth or chunky)
- 2 cups vegetable or chicken broth
- 2 tablespoons vegetable oil
- 1 tablespoon tomato paste
- 1 teaspoon ground cayenne pepper (adjust to taste)
- 1 teaspoon ground ginger
- Salt and pepper to taste
- Fresh cilantro or parsley, chopped, for garnish
- Cooked rice or fufu (cassava or plantain dough), for serving

Instructions:

1. **Brown the Meat:**
   - Heat vegetable oil in a large pot or Dutch oven over medium-high heat.
   - Add the meat cubes and brown them on all sides. Remove from the pot and set aside.
2. **Sauté Aromatics:**
   - In the same pot, add chopped onion and sauté until softened and translucent, about 5-7 minutes.
   - Add minced garlic and sauté for another 1-2 minutes until fragrant.
3. **Add Tomatoes and Tomato Paste:**
   - Stir in chopped tomatoes and tomato paste. Cook for about 5 minutes until tomatoes break down and release their juices.
4. **Prepare the Peanut Butter Sauce:**
   - Add peanut butter to the pot, stirring continuously to combine with the onion and tomato mixture.
   - Gradually add vegetable or chicken broth, stirring constantly to create a smooth sauce.
5. **Cook the Meat:**
   - Return the browned meat cubes to the pot. Cover and simmer over medium-low heat for about 1 to 1.5 hours, or until the meat is tender and cooked through.
6. **Add Leafy Greens:**
   - Stir in chopped leafy greens (spinach, collard greens, or a combination). Cook for another 10-15 minutes until the greens are wilted and cooked through.
7. **Season and Simmer:**

- Add ground cayenne pepper, ground ginger, salt, and pepper to taste. Adjust seasoning as needed.
- Let the Palava sauce simmer for another 10-15 minutes to allow the flavors to meld together and the sauce to thicken slightly.

8. **Serve:**
   - Garnish Liberia's Palava Sauce with chopped fresh cilantro or parsley before serving.
   - Serve hot over cooked rice or fufu, enjoying the delicious and hearty flavors of this traditional West African dish.

Palava sauce is versatile and can be adapted with different types of meat or even made vegetarian by omitting the meat and using vegetable broth instead. It's a comforting and nutritious meal that is sure to delight with its rich, peanutty sauce and tender greens.

www.ingramcontent.com/pod-product-compliance
Lightning Source LLC
LaVergne TN
LVHW081602060526
838201LV00054B/2024